Structural Power-Dependence and Social Negotiation in Exchange Networks

International Studies in Sociology and Social Anthropology

VOLUME 143

The titles published in this series are listed at *brill.com/issa*

Structural Power-Dependence and Social Negotiation in Exchange Networks

A Research Program in Progress

By

John F. Stolte

BRILL

LEIDEN | BOSTON

Originally published in hardback in 2024.

Cover illustration: John F. Stolte (generated using the Google Gemini program on June 17, 2024).

The Library of Congress Cataloging-in-Publication Data is available online at https://catalog.loc.gov
LC record of the hardback edition available at https://lccn.loc.gov/2024046873

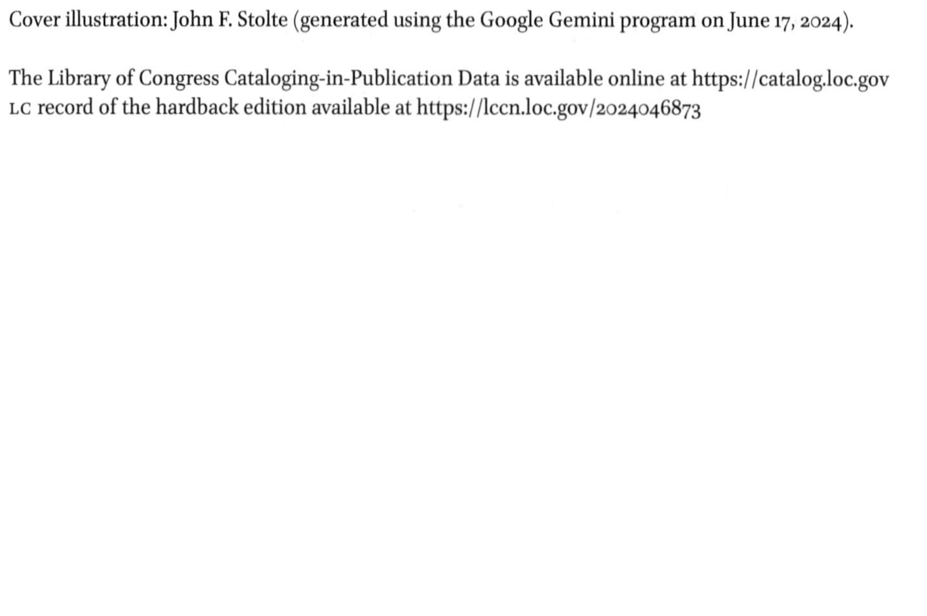

Typeface for the Latin, Greek, and Cyrillic scripts: "Brill". See and download: brill.com/brill-typeface.

ISSN 0074-8684
ISBN 978-90-04-75913-8 (paperback, 2025)
ISBN 978-90-04-71392-5 (hardback)
ISBN 978-90-04-71391-8 (e-book)
DOI 10.1163/9789004713918

This book is printed on acid-free paper and produced in a sustainable manner.

Contents

Preface

Richard Emerson's (1976) review of *social exchange theory* stands out as one of the most perceptive and prescient examinations of a perspective that has stimulated and continues to stimulate much research across the social sciences today. In that review, he traced the background and sketched the likely trajectory of that perspective. He clearly and objectively discussed various conceptual/methodological controversies (e.g., "collective emergence vs. individual reductionism," "subjective, self-interested, rational decision-making" vs. "objectively patterned observable behavior," and "untestable logical tautology" vs. "empirically testable prediction" among others). He noted that such scholarly controversies, have been wide, heated, and persistent. Problematically, and crucially, he argued that such controversies have absorbed too much scholarly focus/time, and therefore have "seriously retarded empirical research" essential for making progress in the field (Emerson, 1976:359).

To contribute to such progress, he formulated a testable systematic theory of social exchange (Emerson, 1969; 1972) that has since gained substantial scholarly attention. At the heart of his formulation was the choice of the "longitudinal social exchange relation" rather than the "individual action/decision" or "separate market transaction" as "the unit of analysis" (Emerson, 1976:359). Also crucial in his formulation was the explicit choice to use entirely objective, Skinnerian operant-behavioral psychology as the conceptual underpinning for understanding the interaction between and among actors in social exchange relations, exchange networks, and groups. Importantly, however, while he expressly chose to limit his theory to this objective behavioral viewpoint, he did not argue that subjective and intersubjective facets of social exchange must always be excluded. Indeed, starting with but building beyond Emerson's theory, the present research monograph intentionally explores and includes subjective and intersubjective facets of social exchange, aiming to significantly enrich our understanding.

References

Emerson, R.M. (1969) Operant psychology and exchange theory. In R.L. Burgess and D. Bushell (eds.) Behavioral Sociology, Columbia University Press.

Emerson, R.M. (1972) Exchange theory: Parts I and II. In J. Berger, M. Zelditch, and B. Anderson (eds.) Sociological Theories in Progress, vol. 2, Houghton Mifflin.

Emerson, R.M. (1976) Social exchange theory. *Annual Review of Sociology* 2:335–62.

Acknowledgements

This monograph has benefitted from inspiration, critical feedback, and help provided to me by many people. First, the advice and support provided by Dick Emerson, my mentor at the University of Washington, was essential. He was supportive and encouraging, but his rigorous standards of independent scholarship were demanding. Under his leadership, I grew professionally. Second, I am grateful for the contact I had with Joe Berger, Buzz Zelditch, and Henry Walker at Stanford University, made possible by a year-long post-doctoral research fellowship funded by the National Institute of Mental Health. From these scholars, I learned why and how to build and test general process theories in social science. Third, I am appreciative of the small grants, research space, and research assistance provided by Northern Illinois University. Especially supportive colleagues at NIU were Professor Gian Sarup, and Professor Shirley Richmond. I am indebted to Dr. Richmond for facilitating my post-NIU scholarly appointment at the University of Texas, MD Anderson, where I was able to continue my research program. Fourth, the collaboration I had with Karen Cook of Stanford University and Gary Fine of Northwestern University was stimulating. Fifth, my professors at San Diego State University, Dale Johnson, Orin Klapp, and Morris Daniels, helped me build a solid foundation in sociology. Sixth, the collaboration I had with Lorraine Belliveau, a master's student at Lakehead University in Canada, and Shanon Fender, a master's student at NIU, helped to expand the research program covered in this book. Seventh, the anonymous reviewers, editors, and staff at DeGruyter-Brill Publishing, especially Jason Prevost, Katie Short, and Carina van den Hoven provided indispensable technical help in the production of this research monograph, and I am deeply grateful. Eighth, and most significantly, I am *profoundly indebted* to Carol Stolte (my wife, who helped to meticulously copy edit this book), Jeff Stolte (my son), and Kris Stolte-Hartmann (my daughter). The unflagging love and support from these three very special people across the years have made the work reported here possible.

PART 1

Introduction and Background

∵

CHAPTER 1

General Process Theories in the Social Sciences

As Ahmed, Nawaz, Ishtiaq, Kahn, and Ashraf (2023:01) have noted: "Social exchange theory (SET) is one of the most influential theories in the social sciences, which has implications across various fields." These authors conducted a meta-analysis of the large, relevant past research literature, showing broad conceptual commonalities across many, varied contributions to this field of study. Such analyses are important, and it is a worthwhile goal to examine and, where possible, synthesize key concepts and principles from the broad literature on social exchange. However, the basic goal of the present monograph is more limited: it is to review past and present studies in one program of research on social exchange, as well as suggest potentially important new directions for future studies in this field.

This research program has been fundamentally shaped by Emerson's (1962; 1969; 1972; 1976; 1981) structural power-dependence theory of social exchange. The starting point for the research program was the experimental study reported by Stolte and Emerson, (1977). That study focused on the nature and dynamics of power-dependence in the context of social exchange networks. It clarified the nature of *positional power-dependence* as a determinant of social stratification. Since its beginning, structural power-dependence has continued to serve as a core theoretical frame for studies thus far conducted in the program. However, this frame has been elaborated, extended, and linked to other sociological and social psychological processes as the program has evolved. Central goals of the current monograph are to (a) review major past developments of this research program, (b) report new research in the program, and (c) point to potentially important future research pathways. Overall, this monograph aims to clarify and describe structural power-dependence as one systematic perspective on core issues addressed in the large research literature on social exchange.

To provide an initial context, we now discuss (a) the nature of *a general process theory* (b) examine a research program on *status characteristics* as one illustration of such a theory, (c) briefly introduce the *research program on structural power-dependence* as a second *illustration* of such a theory, and (d) argue that some of the formal tenants of building a general process theory can and should be relaxed to encourage the incorporation of new theoretical ideas and the use of new methodological tools.

 | DOI:10.1163/9789004713918_002

1 The Character of a General Process Theory

One possible approach to scholarship is to engage in detailed, particularistic, historical research. Among other things, this approach entails a painstaking search for and use of documents and other evidence (written, audio, video, artifactual) to lay out the unique sequence of events, the particular identities of essential participants, and the broader sociohistorical consequences that have occurred in a particular location at a given time in the past. For example, an historian might ask: Why and how did the violent insurrection against the U.S. Capital occur on January 6, 2020? Why and how did members of the UAW call a massive strike against key corporate manufacturers in the U.S. automobile industry in September, 2023? Why do many people today around the globe spend substantial personal time each day posting opinions and personal information (e.g., photos and videos) on various social media platforms? An historian would seek to answer such questions as objectively, and thoroughly as possible, thereby providing a clear historical explanation of the relevant events, participants, and phenomena.

By contrast, an alternative approach to scholarship is to formulate a general process theory and conduct a program of empirical research to test, refine, and extend that theory. Rather than focusing on the myriad of concrete, particular conditions that have occurred in and around some significant social event (such as the riot of January 6, 2020, the union action of September, 2023, or the widespread posting to social media), a scholar might instead work to construct, empirically test, support, and/or revise a general process theory of riots, strikes, or personal media posting behavior. Such a theory would not construe a riot, strike, or media posting as a unique, once-in-a-lifetime set of events/conditions happening in a particular location. Instead, the theory would construe such events/conditions as part of a general process that regularly recurs under specific conditions. A general process theory assumes that events obey law-like principles that can be established empirically and formally stated. Such a theory is based on the assumption that a causal mechanism, simple or complex, lies at the heart of a general process. Once the dynamic principles of the general process are understood theoretically, predictions that follow from those principles can be logically derived and formally stated as hypotheses. The hypotheses can be tested empirically. Procedures can be designed to carefully make controlled observations and collect data. The data can demonstrate whether or not the hypotheses are or are not supported.

A *general process theory* of a riot, a strike, or a tendency to post to social media will be continuously subjected to empirical scrutiny. An ongoing research program of relevant studies will be conducted to test predictions deduced from the evolving theory in progress. Ideally, according to the formal tenants of the methodology of general process theory construction, such studies ought to be controlled experiments. If theoretical principles survive across a program of continuous empirical testing, such principles are retained. If they do not, they are revised and extended. Potentially relevant conditions and dynamics will be carefully monitored and included as dictated by the theory and data as the research program continues. Along the way, novel nuances of relevant knowledge about the event/phenomenon (riot, strike, and media posting) may well arise and become new foci within the theoretical research program. New principles will be formulated to clarify and account for these new bits of data-based knowledge. Overall, the program aims to produce an integrated line of increasingly sophisticated, "cumulative" empirical knowledge. Through such a program of cumulative research, a body of general, logically consistent, empirically verified understanding of a given event/phenomenon (riots, strikes, media posting) can result. It is even possible, in some cases, that a research program pursuing a general process theory will yield some level of control over the event/phenomenon being studied. That is, the resulting knowledge might help shape practical policies and programs, leading to better outcomes for people.

It should be stressed, however, that both these knowledge-gaining strategies, historical analysis and general process theory construction, are legitimate and each can be useful. The two strategies take different tacks to arrive at different forms of "knowing." Each contributes an enriching, deeper level of human understanding. No judgment is made here about which approach is "best" or more "useful." The choice of strategy to follow, if a choice must be made, depends on a scholar's goals.

2 First Example of a General Process: Status Characteristics

An important example of a general process theory is the cumulative experimental research program focused on "*status characteristics*." Here we discuss only the fundamental ideas of this line of work, using relatively non-technical language. For greater detail, see Berger, Anderson, and Zelditch (1972). We base the present discussion on the literature review published by Berger, Rosenholtz, and Zelditch (1980). These authors describe and take stock of the much larger body of related research.

We start with a very important "scope condition." It is explicitly assumed that status characteristics theory will apply only to some kinds of social situations, not others. Specifically, this theory will relate only to a small, face-to-face problem-solving group of people, where the group members have explicitly joined together to help one another successfully solve a problem being confronted by the group. The task is a collective task, calling for one or more collective decisions. The concrete tasks and groups to be explained and understood by this theory might vary. Possible hypothetical examples include (a) an academic committee needing to decide whether or not to expel a student accused of cheating, (b) a mountain-climbing group aiming to scale Mr. Everest, or (c) a small group of young artificial intelligence (AI) technicians aiming to create a ground-breaking and workable artificial intelligence device. Each example can be considered a concrete instance of a "problem-solving group facing a collective task." Members of each group are all motivated to work together so as to make successful group decisions leading to a successful group outcome. Throughout their work together, group members will make a series of significant collective decisions. Such decisions will eventuate in a final outcome decided by the group, whether that outcome is a success or a failure. The committee members who decide to expel the student, but who later find the student innocent of the accusation, will have failed. The Everest climbers who choose an eastern rather than western route up the mountain let us assume succeed. The AI device creators who agree on plan A but not plan B for AI code creation let us assume succeed.

This general process theory centers attention on the effect of *member status characteristics* on the dynamics and results of group problem-solving behavior. Members of such groups can and usually do vary on many different such characteristics: gender, race, class, age, education, mathematical ability, athletic prowess, physical attractiveness, and other personal traits. The academic committee might be composed of a mix of "hard science" faculty members (physics, chemistry, biology), as well as "social science/humanities" faculty members (sociology, psychology, English, Foreign language, Philosophy). The Everest climbing expedition might be composed of some European climbers who have successfully scaled the mountain at least five times before as well as climbers attempting a first climb. The AI device creators might be made up of white male members and black female members.

A given status characteristic is a stereotyped trait: it is widely believed in the broader culture outside of but impinging upon the small problem-solving group to carry certain implications about a group member's nature, ability, and/or propensities. For example, males are often believed to have intrinsically higher mathematical/logical ability than females. Of course, a large amount of actual, objective social scientific evidence consistently shows stereotyped status characteristics, such as "maleness," to be overgeneralized and false.

Nevertheless, erroneous stereotyped beliefs such as this are often taken as true by many people.

Status characteristics theory asserts that variation in the status characteristics that members bring into a problem-solving group is a causal condition that will have predictable consequences for patterns of social interaction among group members. For example, assume the AI device creators are all of equal education, technical skill, and past work experience, but some are male and some are female. Status characteristics theory predicts that this variation is likely to produce a resultant "power and prestige order" favoring male group members. Following the current illustration, the theory predicts that male AI creators, relative to the female creators, will tend to be allocated significantly more/higher "(a) performance opportunities, (b) action/performance outputs, (c) positive group evaluations of action/performance outputs, and (d) influence in the face of disagreements about group decisions" (Berger, Rosenholtz, and Zelditch, 1980, p. 488–489).

Status characteristics theory predicts that regardless of the empirical veracity (or lack of it) in reference to "maleness" vs. "femaleness," the group members will tend to discriminate against female AI creators. Both male and female AI creators may well take the resultant power and prestige order as "legitimate and proper," because "everybody knows" that "males have superior intelligence, mathematical, and coding ability compared to females." If group members become aware of gender differences within the group, participation and influence are (i.e., status is) likely to be allocated unequally in favor of males over females.

As the review by Berger, Rosenholtz, and Zelditch (1980) demonstrates, many experiments using different group problem-solving situations and different stereotyped status characteristics have tested and supported status characteristics theory as a general process.

3 Second Example of a General Process: Structural Power-Dependence

Another illustration of a general process theory, and one that provides the essential backdrop for the present monograph, is Richard M. Emerson's structural power-dependence formulation of social exchange networks. This theory is complex and intricate. To fully appreciate its sociological reach and complex nuances, the reader is urged to carefully examine Emerson's (1962; 1969; 1972; 1976; 1981) original work per se. Here, we will selectively extract, summarize, and illustrate only a subset of the major concepts and principles bearing most directly on the studies and issues pursued in the research program to be examined in the present monograph. We draw especially from ideas advanced originally by Stolte and Emerson (1977).

First, consider Illustration 1 at the bottom of this page.

A and B are individual social actors (person A and person B). Suppose A is a high-level crime boss in the Mafia, and B is a young aspiring member of the crime network. Hypothetically, let us assume that A is very experienced in crime and has amassed substantial wealth in the crime network. A has many valuable material and behavioral resources at her/his disposal that she/he can choose to provide, and B has far fewer resources, mostly obedient behavior in the form of doing A's bidding when asked. Assume A owns an automobile dealership in the local community and appears to the community to be a long-standing, legitimate businessperson. However, suppose A also has an extremely lucrative, hidden drug-running "business." A may request various behavioral resources (e.g., "services") from B. Among such services, let us say, B is asked to regularly and effectively manage A's drug business, seeing to it that other members of the broader criminal mob get drugs and sell them to drug-users in the community. Of course, from A's perspective (and B's) this entire "drug enterprise" must remain completely hidden from non-criminal members of the community, especially members of law enforcement. By providing regular, trustworthy "management actions" to A, actor B regularly transfers rewarding and valued exchange outcomes (especially vast wealth) to A. Let us assume that, in exchange, A regularly pays B handsomely and provides B with expensive gifts (e.g., an expensive new car along with many other perquisites).

In Emerson's theoretical language, the A ... B relationship is an established exchange relationship. It entails an on-going, longitudinal series of transactions in which there is a regular, mutual transfer of valued resources/benefits between actor A and actor B.

Sometimes, within an exchange relationship, mutual resistance can occur. Let us suppose A wants to expand his drug enterprise, and to do so, he asks B to select additional drug-runners and spend much more time in a given

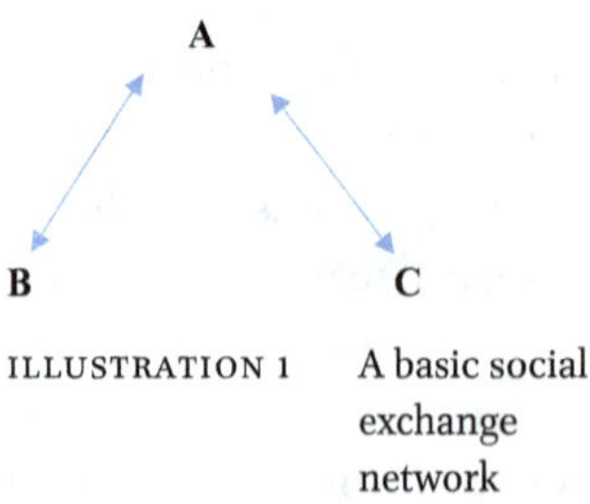

ILLUSTRATION 1 A basic social exchange network

week buying and selling drugs. Problematically, let us assume, B is exhausted and strongly feels she/he is already working up to her/his maximum capacity. Perhaps B complains about A's expectation that B dramatically increase the number of "management actions" B provides to A's enterprise. In an exchange relationship, when mutual "resistance" arises, social power-dependence will begin to operate. For Emerson, (1962) "The power of actor A over actor B is equal to the amount of resistance on the part of B that can be potentially overcome by A" (Emerson, 1962: 32; Emerson, 1972; also see Stolte, 1987).

To understand power dynamics within a social exchange relationship, the *relative dependence of A upon B and B upon A* become important considerations. In this hypothetical example, A is dependent upon B for "management actions" necessary for effectively running the hidden drug business. B is dependent upon A for considerable wealth and material benefits.

In an exchange relation, A depends upon B, and B depends upon A for a variety of valued social exchange outcomes (resources/benefits of many and varied kinds). In Emerson's theory, one crucial determinant of the mutual dependence of actors A and B is the *level of value*, each actor places upon valued resources/benefits obtained through exchange with the other. The greater the value A places on B's management actions, the greater A's dependence on B. And the greater the value B places on the money/perquisites he obtains from A, the greater the dependence of B upon A.

In this general process theory, a second determinant of mutual dependence is *availability*. Let us assume that A can get the drug business management services she/he needs and highly values only from his relationship with B, and let us also assume B can get the highly valued material (economic and other benefits) she/he gets only from A. Under this hypothetical scenario, the A … B exchange relationship is balanced because mutual dependence is *equal and balanced*. Consequently, if and when mutual resistance emerges between A and B, the use of power will be balanced and equal between these two actors. Thus, the net resource value ("exchange ratio") across transactions obtained by A will be equal to the net resource value ("exchange ratio") obtained by B.

However, suppose that mutual dependence in the A … B exchange relationship is not equal. Suppose B depends significantly more upon A than A depends upon B. Suppose A can easily get everything, including the crime enterprise management services she/he currently obtains from B from actor C in the crime network, a young equally aspiring mobster who competes with B to engage in exchange with A. Under this scenario, the A---B exchange relationship is *unequal and imbalanced* in favor of actor A. Further, actor A can be said to have a *power-advantage* due to her/his favored *position in the exchange network*. B and C can get what they need and value only from A, while A can get what she/he needs and values from either B or C.

According to Emerson's power-dependence theory, when actors A and B are linked in an imbalanced exchange relationship, the actor with a power advantage will, across transactions, use that advantage to obtain an increasingly beneficial exchange ratio at the expense of the actor(s) with a power disadvantage, who will correspondingly suffer an increasingly diminished exchange ratio.

Importantly, this theory, by design, omits consideration of what actors A and B might "feel," "know" or "intend (implicitly or explicitly)." The theory (based exclusively on Skinnerian operant-behavioral psychology) asserts that where actors occupy structurally unequal positions, such as those occupied by B and C relative to A, the more power-advantaged actor (A) will use power-advantage to increase the exchange ratio obtained, while power-disadvantaged actors (B and C) will be subject to a decrease in the exchange ratio obtained across transactions. Importantly, this formulation of structural power-dependence does not focus on actors' subjective states (feelings or thoughts). Subjective states and interpersonal meaning construction and communication are excluded as a basic scope condition by the theory. We will return to this point below, showing how it pertains to the research program to be considered in subsequent chapters

One might exclusively follow the formal, limiting dictates of the methodology for developing a general process theory. However, the work covered in the present monograph does not conform strictly to such dictates. Also, one might exclusively take the purely objective stance that Emerson does in building his structural power-dependence formulation upon operant behaviorism. However, the research program considered in this monograph follows a different path. The line of work considered here, by design, has substantially relaxed the methodological requirements and broadened the research purview. Subsequent to the study reported by Stolte and Emerson (1977), the studies covered in this monograph evolved and developed in two general ways. *First*, they expressly expanded the research focus beyond a purely objective behavioral view by explicitly considering the part played by various other facets of social psychology (subjective feelings, cognitions, as well as the interpersonal construction and communication of meanings). *Second*, the studies examined in this monograph have employed empirical research methods that include but go well beyond the controlled laboratory experiment, the method traditionally favored for studying general process theories. Beyond some studies using the controlled laboratory experiment, other studies covered in the present monograph draw data or propose ideas based on the quantitative non-experimental social survey, the vignette/scenario experiment, the qualitative ethnographic case study, psycholinguistic analysis, and purely qualitative theoretical speculation. The position taken here is that the use of different research methods to collect diverse kinds of data for arriving at new ideas enhances the likelihood of attaining a richer, deeper understanding of structural power-dependence and social exchange. In the chapters that follow we show how these developments have allowed new questions to be addressed in different ways.

4 Structural Power-Dependence: A Deeper Dive

We now elaborate the discussion of structural power-dependence by delving more deeply into the importance of the "*positional*" basis of power-dependence in a surrounding social exchange network. Within the many and varied strands of research comprising social exchange theory, as Szmatka and Mazur (1996:274) point out, the study published by Stolte and Emerson (1977) was the first to experimentally demonstrate the causal impact of a truly "social structural" approach to power-dependence dynamics. Stolte and Emerson focused expressly on the impact of an actor's *relative position* in a social exchange network composed of other actors and their relative positions within a wider network, emphasizing that exchange networks might exhibit varying configurations. The broader *network itself*, possibly varying in size and complexity, became the focus of studies reported by "network theorists" across various academic specialties: sociology, social psychology, and behavioral economics. The Stolte/Emerson experiment shifted vision significantly beyond the behavioral dynamics impinging upon an individual actor or a two-party exchange relationship. The vision changed from an actor or dyad to the surrounding social exchange network structure itself, composed of three, four, ... N actors. The social exchange paradigm changed. Research attention, especially among social scientists, shifted from the micro-social toward the macro-social level of theorizing and empirical research.

Apropos of this point, the experiment reported by Stolte (1988) explicitly explored how research might move beyond simple, categorical concepts such as "hi" vs. "low," or "balanced" vs. "Imbalanced," positional power-dependence, concepts limited to the two-party exchange relationship. In contrast, the experiment proposed a *structural level measure*, "dependence differential (DD)" explicitly intended to capture how the exchange network configuration surrounding a given position impacts that position's relative power-dependence. Also, the experiment proposed a *structural level measure*, "exchange ratio stratification (ERSTRAT)" that could be used to demonstrate an exchange network-wide impact of structural power-dependence inequality upon the relative exchange-ratios obtained by advantaged and disadvantaged actors in the exchange network. Using these new operationalizations, the data reported by Stolte (1988) strongly supported theoretical predictions following from Emerson's (1962; 1969; 1972; 1981) theory as well as the original Stolte and Emerson (1977) experiment. What these data added, however, while preliminary, was clear experimental evidence squarely addressing the *structural* level of social exchange. (See study cited for elaboration of the technical details.)

The trajectory begun by the Stolte (1988) research, continues at various points in the research program discussed in the following chapters: a number of questions require consideration of different levels of analysis, from the micro-level toward the macro-level of social exchange network dynamics.

Social exchange networks might be composed of varying configurations of "connections" among actors. A basic contrast is drawn in by Emerson (1969;1972) between "positive" and "negative" connections, as well as "direct" and "indirect" connections among actors in exchange networks. Consider the contrast between three social exchange structures shown in Illustrations 2, 3, and 4.

In reference to the first Illustration, 2, the "Star," (see Stolte and Emerson, 1977, p. 132–133) assume that letters represent practicing physicians in a large metropolitan area. For simplicity, assume that each line represents an established, longitudinal, reciprocal exchange relationship. The same resource, let us say, a "favor" in the form of a patient referral is exchanged between a given pair of doctors. Let us assume the value placed by a doctor upon any favor (patient referral) received is equal. (This assumption is unlikely to hold in the real world. However, a general process theory can *assume it logically* as a meaningful scope condition for purposes of further theory building and empirical testing.) Due to various factors, (e.g., recency of arrival in this metropolitan area, past social contact opportunities, being a new or an established physician in the area etc.), the doctors might occupy different positions in an exchange network.

Hypothetically, in reference to Illustration 2, assume that Doctor A1 regularly obtains favors from either doctor, A2, or A3, or A4. However, A2, A3, and A4 obtain favors only from A1. Under these theoretical conditions, doctor A1 occupies a position of power-dependence advantage in the "star" (labeled a "unilateral monopoly," elsewhere in the research program) while A2, A3, and A4 occupy a position of power-dependence disadvantage. The relative positional power-dependence advantage or disadvantage is determined by the *availability factor* discussed earlier. Whenever "resistance" must be overcome to obtain a favor (e.g., all the doctors are extremely busy and have very limited time, which might well create resistance to allocating a favor/referral when it

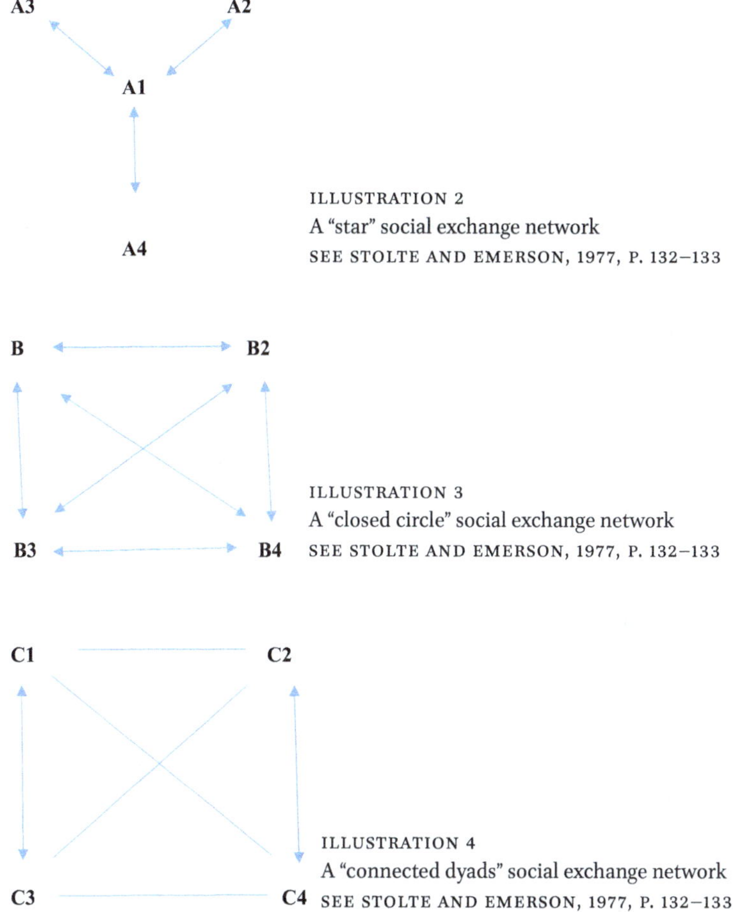

ILLUSTRATION 2
A "star" social exchange network
SEE STOLTE AND EMERSON, 1977, P. 132–133

ILLUSTRATION 3
A "closed circle" social exchange network
SEE STOLTE AND EMERSON, 1977, P. 132–133

ILLUSTRATION 4
A "connected dyads" social exchange network
SEE STOLTE AND EMERSON, 1977, P. 132–133

is expected in any given instance.) Such resistance will tend to be more overcome in favor-providing referrals by the other doctors in the network to doctor A1 than provided by A1 to the other doctors. In short, valued resource benefits ("exchange ratios") in the form of favors (patient referrals), will tend to flow unequally from A2, A3, and A4 to A1.

The "star" or "unilateral monopoly" network entails objective environmental conditions that underlie the essence of "structural inequality" from this perspective. Again, as stressed above, *variation among positions in the exchange structure per se is* considered the locus of power-dependence inequality among the doctors, *not* the individual motivational/personality traits or cognitive/emotional states of the doctors. Structural inequality is seen here as a sociological/emergent ("sui generis") phenomenon. It is not reduced to an individual psychological phenomenon. Modern social psychology, of course, does bridge the emergent structural level and the individual psychological level. At this point we are emphasizing the sociological ("social structural") side of power-dependence. However, subsequent chapters will show how the research program evolved to study the link between the sociological and psychological (i.e., social psychological) sides of social exchange.

In reference to Illustration 3 above, the "closed circle," (see Stolte and Emerson, 1977, p. 132–133) also assume letters represent doctors who trade favors (patient referrals) across time. In this case, by contrast, circumstances have shaped the structure of social exchange such that each doctor, B1, B2, B3, and B4 has equal access for favor exchange with every other doctor in the exchange network. In this case, the structure of social exchange is power-balanced: each doctor has a position of equal positional power-dependence. No doctor is relatively more structurally advantaged than any other doctor. When conditions create "resistance" to providing favors, no doctor is in a position to overcome more such resistance than another. Any "costs" in scarce time associated with making patient referrals will be borne equally across longitudinal transactions among all doctors in the network. Also, resource benefits (patient referrals received) will tend to flow equally from each doctor to every other doctor across transactions in the exchange network. In other words, the "closed social circle" entails conditions creating objective "structural equality." Importantly, in the "closed circle" the sheer frequency of exchange transactions is likely to be approximately equal across all six exchange relationships.

Finally, consider Illustration 4, the "connected dyads" exchange network (again, see Stolte and Emerson, 1977, p. 132–133). In this social exchange structure, pairs of doctors have formed relatively exclusive exchange relations. Doctors C1 and C3, on the one hand, and C2 and C4 regularly transact favor/referral exchange, but C1 and C2 or C3 and C4 rarely, if ever, engage one another in such exchange. The lines without arrow heads indicate essentially non-existent significant exchange. The doctors might meet in various contexts and pass the time briefly in friendly, superficial conversation. Such interactions will have virtually no important consequences in terms of the transfer of valued favors/referrals. For reasons outlined above, the relationship between C1 and C3 and the relationship between C2 and C4 will tend to evince structural power-dependence equality/balance. Mutual resistance experienced and mutual power exercised will be likely to even out longitudinally across transactions.

Importantly, the illustrations discussed above direct attention *beyond the individual actor's position* toward the *surrounding configuration of exchange relations within an exchange network.* Again, we emphasize that the discussion

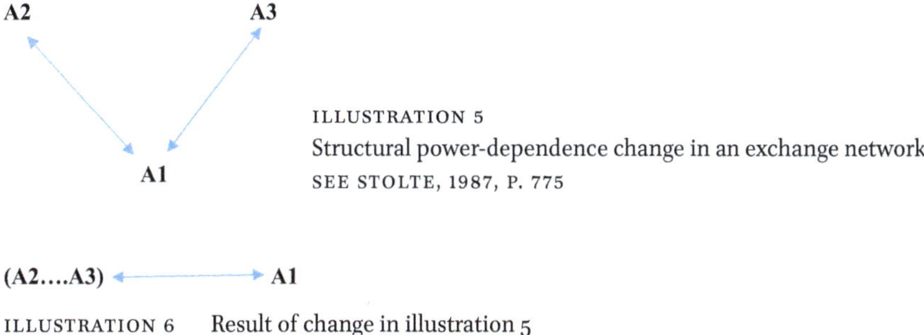

ILLUSTRATION 5
Structural power-dependence change in an exchange network
SEE STOLTE, 1987, P. 775

ILLUSTRATION 6 Result of change in illustration 5

so far omits from consideration what actors might be aware of or might feel. Theoretical attention remains exclusively focused on the objective causal impact of relative positional power-dependence as determined by the surrounding exchange structure.

Remaining within this entirely objective perspective, we now consider additional ramifications of structural power-dependence and its use in social exchange networks, drawing from a study reported by Stolte (1987:774–777). Exchange structures not only configure inequality and equality of power-dependence and power use, they also shape objectively available (but perhaps entirely subjectively unknown) potential opportunities for *change* from power-dependence inequality toward equality and back again in a potentially ongoing dialectic across time. This study focused attention on how disadvantaged actors in an unequal power-dependence/social exchange structure might, through structural happenstance, have positions and relations that make it objectively possible for structural change to occur in the surrounding determinants of power-dependence. Certain changes, were they to occur, would objectively modify the distribution of valued resource outcomes ("exchange ratios") achievable by actors in the structure. Stolte (1987:775) discusses an illustration.

Consider the first diagram in Illustration 5 showing a structurally unequal exchange network.

In this structure, as noted above, actor A1 occupies an advantaged power-dependence position in relation to actors A2 and A3. Looked at strictly through an objective lens, *a theorist can see* that the exchange structure might potentially change into a quite different exchange structure, as depicted in the structural change shown in the contrast between Illustrations 5 and 6. From a strictly objective standpoint, were this change to occur, A2 and A3 would come to form a single unit vis-à-vis A1. The terms of social exchange ("exchange ratios") heretofore obtained by A2 and A3 could change, under these conditions, in a favorable direction, from inequality toward equality vis-à-vis A1. And a general process theorist might confine focus to the strictly objective structural power-dependence dynamics, charting such changes from inequality toward equality as they might potentially occur within social exchange networks of varying configuration.

However, the purely objective standpoint discussed thus far shifted significantly in the study reported by Stolte (1987). New questions were posed. In general, those questions derived from a consideration of the *subjective side of each actor's experience* of structural power-dependence and the dynamics of structural change in social exchange networks. In the next chapter, we explicitly include actors' subjective experiences (cognitions, feelings) as well as the interpersonal construction and communication of meanings between and among actors. Also, we will show how this change of theoretical standpoint led to the study of significant new questions using new research methods.

References

Ahmad, R., Nawaz, M.R., Ishaq, M.I., Khan, M.M., and Ashraf, H.A. (2023) Social exchange theory: Systematic review and future directions. *Front. Psychol.* 13:1015921. doi: 0.3389/fpsyg.2022.1015921.

Berger, J., Rosenholtz, S. and Zelditch, M. (1980) Status organizing processes. *Annual Review of Sociology* 6,1:479–508.

Berger, J., Zelditch, M., Anderson, B., and Cohen, B. (1972) Structural aspects of distributive justice: A status value formulation. In J. Berger, M. Zelditch, and B. Anderson (eds.) Sociological Theories in Progress, vol. 2, Houghton Mifflin.

Emerson, R.M. (1962) Power-dependence relations. *American Sociological Review* 27:31–40.

Emerson, R.M. (1969) Operant psychology and exchange theory. In R.L. Burgess and D. Bushell (eds.) Behavioral Sociology, Columbia University Press.

Emerson, R.M. (1976) Social exchange theory. *Annual Review of Sociology* 2:335–62.

Emerson, R.M. (1981) Social exchange theory. In M. Rosenberg and R. Turner (eds.) Social Psychology: Sociological Perspectives, 30–65. Basic Books.

Emerson, R.M. (1972) Exchange theory: Parts I and II. In J. Berger, M. Zelditch, and B. Anderson (eds.) Sociological Theories in Progress, vol. 2, Houghton Mifflin.

Stolte, J.F. (1987) The formation of justice norms. *American Sociological Review* 52,6: 774–784.

Stolte, J.F. (1988) From micro- to macro-exchange structure: Measuring power imbalance at the exchange network level. *Social Psychology Quarterly* 51:357–364.

Stolte, J.F. & Emerson, R. (1977) Structural Inequality: Position and Power in Network Structures. In R. Hamblin & J. Kunkel, Behavioral Theory in Sociology, New York: Transaction Books.

Szmatka, J. and Mazur, J. (1996) Orienting strategies, working strategies, and theoretical research programs in social exchange theory. *Polish Sociological Review*, 265–288.

CHAPTER 2

Structural Power-Dependence Research: Transitions and Developments

As noted above, the early research on structural power-dependence emphasized in Chapter 1 evolved in significant new directions, examined in this chapter. Following the Stolte/Emerson (1977) experiment, several studies built from but moved substantially beyond Emerson's behavioral-structural theory. They addressed new social psychological processes linked to the structure, process, and outcomes of exchange. The program shifted focus to explore links between structural power-dependence and important dimensions of social cognition, affect, and motivation. The program was extended both theoretically and methodologically. (The reader is encouraged to examine the original studies briefly reviewed in this chapter for greater conceptual and methodological detail.)

1 Incorporating Symbolic Interaction Theory

The most significant general shift in the research program was drawing an explicit link between symbolic interaction theory and Emerson's behavioral-structural theory (Stolte, 1987a; also see Singelmann, 1972; Mutran and Reitzes, 1984). As elaborated below, this theoretical extension opened for explicit consideration important interpersonal and individual social psychological dynamics connected to social exchange and structural power-dependence.

We begin by elaborating the illustrations of exchange networks outlined in the previous chapter (see Chapter 1 Illustrations 1, 2, 3, 4, 5, and 6). As noted there, a given structural situation might well *objectively allow for* profound change in the structure of power-dependence relationships via the establishment of new exchange relations and the formation of new coalitions among some actors in relation to other actors. An outside observer might appraise an exchange network situation and see opportunities for structural changes that would benefit the actors ensconced directly within that structural situation. The opportunity for such structural change is determined by complex network configurations of actors and their objective social exchange behavior. But even if such conditions create an objective opportunity for structural change, a new question arises: do the actors themselves (in addition to an objective

 | DOI:10.1163/9789004713918_003

observer) see that opportunity? If those actors see the opportunity, do they use it to effectively mobilize such structural change? Exactly how might the actors who are ensconced within the structural situation at hand become aware and engaged, both as individuals and interpersonally, to actively mobilize such change? To answer such questions, we must theoretically and empirically step into the "subjective and intersubjective" processes activated within and between the actors in a social exchange network. As detailed in Stolte (1987a), we can take such steps by explicitly incorporating insights and assumptions of symbolic interaction theory. Such insights and assumptions were originally contributed by scholars such as Mead, 1934; Cooley, 1922; Berger and Luckman, 1967; Goffman, 1959; Vygotsky, 1962; Luria, 1981; Creelman, 1966; Rommetviet et al., 1979.

Symbolic interactionist insights build upon but substantially expand the behavioral-structural assumptions of Emerson's exchange theory. These insights prompt a number of important new questions. They expand understanding of the subtle connections among the psychological and social dynamics of structural power-dependence and exchange. As Stolte (1987a: 774) put it, to link symbolic interaction and structural exchange is to explore the intricate connections between "ideal" (subjective) and "material" (objective) conditions of social life.

For example, consider again the structural situation discussed in Chapter 1 regarding Illustration 5. Again, ponder the objective power-dependence imbalance shown there among A2 ... A1 ... A3. By virtue of network position, A1 can extract an increasingly favorable exchange ratio, causing a corresponding lowering of exchange ratios obtained by A2 and A3. However, the situation can change fundamentally if A2 and A3 "discover" one another, communicate implicitly or explicitly with one another, and form a mutually meaningful, acceptable, and operative agreement with one another to exchange with A1 only under certain jointly agreed upon conditions. Mutual communication might set the stage for such an agreement. A2 and A3 might start by mutually expressing complaints about their respective exchange ratios. As communication continues, these two actors might gradually arrive at the joint judgment that the existing exchange situation is both punishing and definitely "unfair and improper." In short, A2 and A3 might engage in symbolically mediated, language-based, interpersonal "give-and-take." Using such symbolic interaction capacities, they might engage in a sort of "social negotiation" through which they discover important objective facts comprising the surrounding exchange situation. Further, they might "socially construct" (Berger and Luckman, 1967) and behaviorally mobilize a shared plan to change those objective facts. Beyond a practical joint action plan, these actors might also jointly create a clear justification for their joint plan composed of elaborate reasons. In short, they might negotiate a meaning agreement stipulating that a change in the exchange structure can and should be made. Hence, they might form a joint, mutually coordinated, effective social coalition (shown in Illustration 6). By so doing, they would transform themselves from separate individual actors into a cooperative "collective actor" (a social coalition or group). With this change, actors A2 and A3 would work together to achieve relatively higher exchange ratios. Their respective exchange ratios might soon match A1's exchange ratio. By socially constructing shared meanings in the process of forming a "collective actor," actors A2 and A3 would objectively *balance* structural power-dependence in relation to A1. Put differently, the reciprocal symbolic expression of certain "ideals" occurring between A2 and A3 would cause consequential changes in their "material outcomes" in relation to A1.

Connecting symbolic interaction and structural power-dependence opens up a much broader plane of scientific inquiry. This new, more inclusive focus introduces what actors know, feel, intend, calculate, intuit, and judge. The various ways subjective and intersubjective factors work with objective structural conditions causing structural stabilization or change can be explored. This theoretical expansion gives impetus to the systematic exploration of important new social psychological dynamics. Blending objective-behavioral processes with subjective/intersubjective processes provides a new pathway for research on structural power-dependence and exchange.

Before moving forward, as an important side-note, it is important to distinguish *what* social actors communicate, that is the meaning *content* or substance of their communication, on the one hand, and *how* they communicate, that is, the *process* of communication through which such content is socially constructed and transmitted, on the other hand. Not always, but frequently, this process of communication takes the form of *social negotiation* (Zartman 1977; 2022; Strauss, 1978). Often, some form and amount of social "give-and-take" between or among actors in reference to the surrounding situation will be necessary in order for a final meaning/action agreement to be reached. For example, A2 and A3 might well need to share and clarify information regarding their respective exchange ratios and their respective experiences with and judgments about A1, before either can or will agree to the terms of a final agreement. The research program covered in the present monograph has typically referred to this communication process as *social negotiation.* Clearly such "give and take" will be "dialogical" (Markova, 1982; 2016). It will entail the complex subjective and intersubjective means through which actors confront disputes and work together to resolve them through compromise, finally arriving at a final agreement that is mutually acceptable, binding, and effective.

To illustrate how the linking of symbolic interaction theory and structural power-dependence theory led to the study of new issues using new research methods, we move next to a brief synopsis and overview of selected studies previously published within the research program.

2 Social Norm Formation

Expanding the above discussion (and still focusing on Illustration 6), we must point out that the joint agreement between A2–A3 to form a coalition to balance power-dependence in relation to A1, is technically *not a social norm,* from a sociological perspective. The A2–A3 agreement does not constitute "*legitimate authority*" to which the two actors owe obedience. While the A2–A3 agreement may be mutually seen from each actor's standpoint as positive and self-interest-serving (producing a better exchange ratio for each), it is merely a joint interpersonal agreement, and therefore lacks moral legitimacy standing above both A2 and A3. This point derives from Wolf's (1950) exegesis of Georg Simmel's classic sociology. Simmel noted that an essential element for the establishment of an authoritative, legitimate, social norm is that such a norm stands above each individual actor within a "collective actor," being apprehended by those actors as a "sup*er-individual external facticity.*" That is, a norm must have acquired a social reality beyond and above any individual actor, being anchored in and shared by the members of a *social group*. That is, each actor (A2 and A3 in this illustration) must be confronted by a social group (*an external collective actor*), the members of which all subscribe to and are prepared to stand together in sanctioning obedience to the norm. Hence, in the illustration, in order for one to assume that the new agreement reached through communication is *an authoritative social norm*, at a minimum, actor A1 along with A2 and A3 will need to have joined the coalition/group. In short, the new A2–A3 agreement will need to be ratified and backed by actor A1 also. Were such ratification to occur, a new group composed of three actors will have formed (the parentheses shown in Illustration 6 would need to be re-drawn as follows: (A1, A2, and A3)). At this point, each actor will have become subject to a unified social policy (a social norm), now governing the action-decisions of each individual within the collective actor (coalition; group). As an end result, the previous power-dependence imbalanced social exchange network will be transformed into a new and different structure: a power-dependence balanced collective actor (coalition; group), with a new norm governing the exchange ratio considered acceptable for each actor.

Moving ahead, we now draw attention to a crucial theoretical contrast made within Emerson's behavioral-structural exchange theory (1969; 1972; 1976; 1981). It is the contrast between a "*distributive exchange network*," on the one hand, and a "*productive exchange group*" on the other hand. Actors related to one another within a "distributive exchange network," are bound together in *competitive* social exchange relations, while actors *related* to one another within a "productive exchange group," by contrast, are linked together in *cooperative* social exchange relations. (See Stolte, 1987b for an early experimental study conceptualizing and operationalizing a productive/cooperative network of social exchange.)

For illustration, again consider Illustration 5. As shown in that Illustration, A1, A2, and A3 compose a *distributive/competitive exchange network*. Assume A2 makes computer chips. Actor A3 also makes essentially the same kind of computer chips. Each of these actors is motivated to sell computer chips to A1, who assembles computers from the chips for sale in the computer market. Assume each actor in the exchange network is strongly motivated to maximize profit and minimize cost. Actor A1 is motivated to establish and maintain an exchange relation with A2 and A3, who are intense competitors, whether or not they fully understand this fact or have feelings about this fact. Individually, each actor aims to maximize the attractiveness and value of the chip produced, while minimizing the cost of such production. A2 and A3 each acts vigorously to draw A1 into an exchange relation by outdoing the other in any way that helps attain their respective material goals. Assume that A1 occupies a positional power-dependence advantage in relation to A2 and A3. Assume A1 can get computer chips equally from either A2 or A3 that meet A1's profit-cost goals. But assume that A2 and A3 can sell computer chips only to A1. Then A1 can and likely will, across transactions, obtain computer chips netting a relatively higher profit and lower cost (netting a relatively more positive exchange ratio) than actors A2 or A3. This situation entails the use of an objectively more favorable power-dependence position in the network, as discussed earlier. At the center of this power-dependence dynamic is competition between A2 and A3. As the exclusive buyer of computer chips, actor A1 occupies a "monopolistic position" in the exchange network (or a condition described by Stolte and Emerson, 1977, as a "unilateral monopoly.")

Suppose, however, that A2 and A3 discover their joint profit/cost disadvantage relative to A1 through joint communication and planning (symbolic interaction). Suppose they "put their heads together" creatively, being strongly motivated to solve the problems they jointly face. Suppose they accurately discern that their joint competitiveness is at the heart of their joint exchange ratio problem. Suppose they discover that by "dividing the labor" (Durkheim,

1964) in this exchange network, their profit/cost outcomes will dramatically improve. Changes depicted in the comparison of Illustrations 5 and 6 exemplify the emergence of a norm-bound "division of labor." Assume that within the structure shown in that figure, the condition of "competitive-distribution" is transformed into a "cooperative-production." Assume that within this emergent new exchange structure, A2 starts a new enterprise based on mining and delivering a scarce metal known to be essential for manufacturing computer chips. Assume that A3 becomes strongly motivated to obtain and use this scarce metal which can now be obtained from A2 to improve the quality of chips produced. A1 becomes even happier with the quality of chips now available for assembling computers. With such changes, the behavioral-structural exchange network is transformed: instead of letting competition be the overriding condition, A1, A2, and A3 interact cooperatively to produce computers from their respective resources. With such a change, A1, A2, and A3 are transformed into a collective actor (coalition; group) based on cooperative production. Each produces/contributes a unique resource (chips, scarce metal, computers) within a collective process yielding a better, more favorable, exchange ratio (profit/cost) for each actor.

Stolte (1987a) theorizes that symbolic interaction within varying underlying conditions of structural power-dependence leads to the formation of varying *norms of justice*. (Also see Meeker, 1971; Eckhoff, 1974; Emerson, 1962; 1976; and Stolte, 1987a for a deeper, more complete discussion of the conditions likely to lead to the formation of different justice norms.)

One such justice norm might be: *equality*. Were it to emerge, it would stipulate that for each member of the social group (collective actor) bound by it: a group-relevant action contributed by any member ought to result in an exchange ratio equal to the exchange ratio achieved by any other member of the group contributing a group-relevant action. Continuing the simple illustration above, assume A1, A2, and A3 have divided the labor in the production of computers as described above. If the justice norm, "equality" were to prevail, it would stipulate that an actor should obtain a net exchange ratio (in profit/cost) equal to that obtained by each other group member. If this norm of "equality" does indeed prevail, it is taken as legitimate, and it will be systematically supported via sanctioning, by each group member, A1, A2, and A3.

An alternative justice norm, *equity*, might form among actors A1, A2, and A3 instead. Such a norm, were it to arise and operate, would specify that each member of the group (collective actor) should get an exchange ratio proportional to the value of the group-relevant contribution that actor makes. Under this norm, assume that A2's mining and provision of a very scarce and essential metal for producing computer chips is deemed by everyone to be relatively more valuable in the computer chip production process than either A3's chip-making or A1's computer-assembling, which are seen as of equal value in the production process. A2 therefore ought to get an exchange ratio that is proportionately greater/higher than A3 or A1, both of whom should get an equal exchange ratio. Again, if this justice norm of equity is accepted as a legitimate social norm, it will be supported and sanctioned as binding in governing the exchange ratio outcomes obtained by A1, A2, and A3.

A third possible justice norm that might alternatively form within the structural-behavioral situation at hand is *need*. This norm, were it to develop, would require that a given actor (group member) obtain a level of exchange ratio meeting that actor's need, regardless of that actor's contributed group-relevant action. For example, assume A2, A3, and A1 have divided labor around computer chip production. Assume further that heretofore a justice norm of equality has prevailed. Due to the success of this division of labor, each actor has been able to obtain an exchange ratio that is quite favorable and equal. Suppose, however, that actor A1 suddenly falls seriously ill. If at all possible, for as long as it takes A1 to recover from the illness, a justice norm of need would stipulate that A2 and A3 will do what is necessary to provide an exchange ratio that meets A1's need. For that period of time A1 will not be required to make a group-relevant action contribution. In effect, a justice norm of need specifies that actors A2, and A3, will provide a charitable donation to A1. (Realistically, of course, the absence due to illness of A1's group-relevant action (computer assembling), sooner or later, is likely to make the entire group production enterprise unsustainable. But as long as it is sustainable, the justice norm, "need," will be taken as legitimate by all actors in governing the distribution of relative exchange ratios among actors A1, A2, and A3.)

3 Self-Efficacy

An important contribution to social psychology is Bandura's (1977) cognitive-social learning theory of self-efficacy. As Gecas (1989) noted: "Reviewing the research on self-efficacy one gets the strong impression that high self-efficacy is good to have." His review is scoping, including Bandura's work but also drawing upon a large related body of studies reported by sociologists, psychologists, political scientists, and health researchers. For an individual actor to have high self-efficacy is to have a sense of agency, control, and competence within the wider environment, whether that environment entails family, friendship circle, school, work, or another environment. To have high self-efficacy is to have a cognitive, emotional, and motivational outlook that is positive, optimistic, energetic and engaged. To have high self-efficacy is to be vibrantly linked with various facets of everyday social life. High self-efficacy implies resilience and the ability to confront and solve problems as they arise, persistently even in the face of occasional failures. High self-efficacy implies being attracted to challenges, seeking new opportunities to find solutions and get tasks done effectively. High self-efficacy implies self-confidence in the face of continuing task demands. A high self-efficacy actor relishes the interactive give-and-take of social exchange, because that actor anticipates a relatively high probability of success in achieving positive outcomes. Evidence shows that actors with high self-efficacy tend to be relatively successful in education, occupation, and other areas of achievement in social life. On balance, an actor with relatively high self-efficacy tends to be generally happy and fulfilled.

Of course, by logical implication and a large body of empirical evidence, an actor who suffers low self-efficacy tends to exhibit behavior and achieve outcomes opposite in direction from the behavior and outcomes described above. As a general social psychological condition, low self-efficacy is associated with a sense of "powerlessness, meaningless, normlessness, isolation, and self-estrangement," as Seeman (1959) classically described "alienation."

Importantly, research evidence has established that an actor might have relatively high self-efficacy in some social settings and low self-efficacy in others. It is important to avoid overgeneralizing this core individual quality. However, in some range of cases, having a global sense of either high or low self-efficacy is possible. It seems reasonable to think that it is in such generally extreme social situations that self-efficacy, either high or low, will have the most significant effects on other personal qualities/conditions/emotions/motivations/cognitions (positive or negative).

An experiment reported by Stolte (1978a) brings structural power-dependence theoretically to bear as a key determinant of self-efficacy. This study demonstrates a chain of effects of the position that actor occupies in a structure of power-dependence on self-efficacy. Position-determined relative success or failure in negotiating favorable outcomes of social exchange were shown to shape that actor's self-perceptions. An actor located in a structurally advantaged position tends to see the self as significantly more powerful and more competent/capable than an actor located in a structurally disadvantaged position. The results of this experiment tie to the much larger body of evidence collected by many other scholars and studies showing similar results (Gecas, 1989).

The study by Stolte (1978a), considered in the context of the large body of evidence on self-efficacy, supports the goal of building beyond an exclusively behavioral-structural power-dependence theory. Many important issues and topics at the micro-social, meso-social, and macro-social levels of society turn upon an understanding of the impact of the social psychology of the individual actor within a behavioral-structural power-dependence situation.

Consider a hypothetical illustration of how structural power-dependence might impact self-efficacy. For simplicity we continue to use the A1, A2, A3 … exchange network notation shown in Chapter 1, Illustration 5, but now we vary the hypothetical social setting and actors. Suppose A1 is a 16-year-old boy, and A2 is his mother. There is no father in this situation. A2 has a very hard life. She works long hours for low wages, and she has an alcohol abuse problem, making her unable to provide focused, effective parenting for socializing A1, the teenage boy. Growing and developing across his childhood until his current age, A1, might well have found few consistent opportunities to achieve a generally high sense of self-efficacy within his family. That is, A2 has not systematically provided A1 age-appropriate tasks and behavioral expectations within the family. Within this situation A2 (the mother) has not required A1 (the teenage boy) to regularly perform common tasks within and outside of the family. A1 (the teenage boy) has not been shaped to conform to commonly held cultural expectations through the regular, consistent allocation of behavior-contingent rewards for task successes by A2 (the mother).

Consequently, as time goes by, A1 (the boy) fails to develop a sense of growing efficacy in solving common task problems most youth his age have learned to solve successfully. Overall, in the context of his family (and other typical settings outside the family such as school, neighborhood etc.), A1 might feel relatively incompetent and powerless to produce beneficial outcomes in social exchange. A1 has low self-efficacy not only in relation to his mother, A2, but also in relation to his teacher, the neighbors, as well as others encountered outside the home. Within those social contexts, A1 might actually feel a high level of futility and "alienation."

Suppose, however, A1 meets and establishes an exchange relationship with A3, another boy his age in the neighborhood. Suppose A1 gradually gets connected to A3's network of social exchange including actors (other same-age boys) A4, A5, and A6. Assume A3, A4, A5, and A6 are members of a juvenile gang. (Note these additional actors, A4, A5, and A6 are not depicted in Chapter 1, Illustration 5.) A1's entry into and acceptance by this gang might open to him opportunities for different sorts of actions and action-contingent feedback/exchange outcomes, through which he can gain an increase in his sense of self-efficacy. Suppose A1 gains a relatively high sense of power and competence by proving to be the toughest, fiercest fighter in the gang network against the members of competing gangs in the area. Within the gang, A1 regularly acquires the various satisfactions associated with high self-efficacy (control, engagement, self-confidence). Despite the fact that the gang engages in illegal behavior (e.g., theft, violence, drug running, etc.), A1 is happier and more committed to regular task-solutions within the gang than he is within his own family, school, or neighborhood.

Research (including the study reported by Stolte, 1978a) has shown the causal link between exchange network position and self-efficacy to be important. This causal link might be shown through additional research to account for varying kinds of "success" or "failure" across many social settings.

4 Agency vs. Communion

Bakan (1966) originated the fundamental contrast between "agency" and "communion," two crucial dimensions of individual human existence. In describing this contrast, Saragovi et al. (1997:593) state: "agency refers to urges of self-affirmation and individualization, and it involves self-protection, self-assertion, and self-expansion. Communion, on the other hand, refers to the merging of the individual in a larger social unit and involves cooperation, caring and forming connections with others." Helgeson (1994) draws from the literature contrasting agency and communion, linking it to important differences between women and men. She argues and shows empirical support for the proposition that men tend to be shaped through socialization to lean toward agency, while women are shaped to bend toward communion. That is, social learning within the culture tends to produce men who generally "focus on self and separation." By contrast, such cultural learning tends to create women who typically "focus on others and connection" (Helgeson, 1994:414).

Many scholars, including Saragovi et al. (1997) and Helgeson (1994) have studied the implications of these two fundamental social psychological dimensions for physical and psychological well-being. While the details of this body of research, are complex and nuanced, the evidence in general supports the conclusion that an individual actor tends to have a relatively higher level of over-all wellbeing (physically and psychologically), if that actor achieves *a balance between these two human qualities*. Evidence suggests both qualities are required in some degree, depending on the surrounding situation. Both qualities are necessary for achieving certain important outcomes. To some degree, an actor needs to enact *agency*, serving the self, so as to acquire a sufficient level of necessary positive outcomes (e.g., success in school and at work, earning sufficient money). To some degree, an actor also needs to enact *communion*, serving the needs of other people, so as to obtain a sufficient level of different necessary positive outcomes (e.g., benefits of sharing empathic, trusted, close social connections/bonds). As the cited authors have put it: agency must be "mitigated" by communion, which in turn must be "mitigated" by agency across time and the situations that compose social life, for optimal human functioning/well-being. Being extremely or even exclusively "agentic" or being extremely or even exclusively "communal" can be deleterious to both functioning and well-being.

A study within the present research program (Stolte, 2000) explicitly focused on agency vs. communion. This study undertook a secondary analysis of an archive of nationally representative social survey data made available by the National Opinion Research Center (University of Chicago). The time-frame covered was 1974–1994. The study focused on survey items measuring "trends in the value placed by Americans on socially extrinsic ("agentic") vs. intrinsic ("communal") outcomes of social exchange" (Stolte, 2000:387). Consistently, these macro-level social survey data showed that across the years in question the value placed on extrinsic/agentic outcomes (specifically income) increased. Conversely, the data showed that from 1974 through 1994, the value placed on "intrinsic/communal" outcomes (specifically outcomes mediated by marriage, kin contact, neighborly interaction, fraternal and/or church membership) decreased. Based on this evidence, and the previous analyses reported by Helgeson, (1994) and Saragovi et al. (1997), Stolte (2000) raised this question: were Americans, during the 1974–1994-time frame exhibiting an *imbalance* in the value placed on "extrinsic/agentic" outcomes at the expense of the value placed on "intrinsic/communal" outcomes of social exchange? Were Americans subject to various ill-effects on their overall well-being of such an imbalance? Of course, far more data would be needed to answer these questions definitively, but the data are suggestive. A worthwhile goal for future research might be to explore these issues in greater depth.

This discussion can be linked back to some of the ideas/findings covered earlier in this chapter. Bakan's (1966) contrast between agency and communion can be linked to Emerson's (1969; 1972) contrast between a *distributive/competitive power-dependence structure* and a *productive/cooperative power-dependence structure* discussed above. Clearly, it would be in the dynamics of a distributive/competitive structure that social exchange among actors would be motivated primarily by agency. Actors located within such a situation would expect and be expected to act and interact vis-à-vis one another based on a vigorous self-interested, competitive pursuit of positive outcomes. By contrast, it would be in the dynamics of a productive/cooperative structure that social exchange would be motivated, to a significant degree, by communion. The same actors at different times and places, of course, might be linked in either a distributive/competitive or a productive/cooperative situation.

Which structural situation, and which basic modality, agency vs. communion, emerges at a given time and place will depend upon social situational "framing," a topic examined below.

Also, we note a link between Bakan's (1966) principle, "communion," and the formation of the particular justice norm, "need," discussed above. Within a productive/cooperative exchange structure, actors might be oriented toward both working together to obtain extrinsic/agentic outcomes (success/money), but also may have formed a connection socially, a bond of mutual communal caring. Hence, they may, to some degree, subordinate their joint pursuit of extrinsic/agentic outcomes. They may, as in the earlier example, implement a social justice norm stipulating that a given actor's exchange ratio will be provided based upon that actor's need.

Clearly, the two principles, agency and communion, are both relevant to an understanding of structural power-dependence. Much exchange theory seems to focus primarily (even exclusively) on the extrinsic/agentic side of social exchange. It is a widespread notion in some approaches to social exchange that the human actor is always and only "rationally self-interested." The present program of research disputes this limited view. Human actors, we contend, often engage one another in a dynamic dialectic: sometimes they engage competitively in transactions characterized mainly as extrinsic/agentic; sometimes they engage cooperatively in transactions characterized primarily as intrinsic/communal. The exact conditions underlying and explaining the changes that unfold within this dialectic need to be explored and explained more fully. One important step in such exploration/explanation entails the topic of social situational "framing," which explains some important conditions governing the agency-communion dialectic.

5 Framing Social Situations and Social Values

Tirolians and Gaskell (2011) have contributed an important synthesis of the social psychological literature on social values. As these authors (2011: 2) say, "values ... arise out of human experience ... and allow the evaluation of states and situations and guide behavior" (Williams and Albert, 1990:286). Various complex facets of social values have been studied by sociologists, psychologists, and cultural anthropologists from the 1930's to the present day. Scholars have focused on many different ways to conceptualize, measure, and theoretically explain the causes and effects of such values. One important insight that has arisen from previous research is that social life, as lived day-to-day by the individual, is very pluralistic: as an actor moves through any given day, that actor will invariably encounter quite divergent social settings/situations, will invariably encounter quite different others who display actions based on diverse social values. Contradictions and conflicts among and between expected and enacted social values are extremely probable and quite frequent. The human self, adaptively moving through daily life, will necessarily act in a "dialogical" manner (Markova, 1982; 2016; Hermans, 1996). That is, the human self will frequently be confronted by the need to socially negotiate "value trade-offs." It is important to examine the variation in the social contexts that arise, because "values … are elements that are dynamically constructed in relationship with others" (Tirolians and Gaskell 2011:18).

Within the research program covered in the present monograph, the experiment reported by Stolte and Fender (2007) pursues the issue of "value tradeoffs" from the perspective of *social situational framing*. This core idea draws importantly from the ground-breaking contributions of Erving Goffman to symbolic interaction theory. As this theorist argued (Goffman, 1974: 45), "framing transforms the meaning of a social situation." A given social frame derives, in part, from an "already meaningful (cultural) schema for interpretation (p. 45)." A schema is an internalized cultural framework which can be activated by concrete "cues" or "primers" that an actor encounters as she/he enters a given social situation. In effect, such cues "tell" the actor which social value out of various alternative sets of values should be heeded as a guide for thinking, feeling, and acting in the situation at hand. Following Sewell (1999: 35–61), Stolte and Fender (2007) posited that an individual actor is often required to move through the "complex cultural mosaic, composed of intrinsic (communal) vs. extrinsic (agentic) value frameworks." That is, complex, plural, sometimes contradictory and conflicting social situations arise, requiring that the actor engage in significant "value tradeoffs." Stolte and Fender reported experimental data supporting specific hypotheses suggested by these theoretical ideas on how varying culturally meaningful "cues" or "primers" operate to frame whether an intrinsic/communal or extrinsic/agentic social value will emerge to govern the interaction and social exchange that ensues within a given social situation. The communal vs. agentic character of an experimental narrative, the high or low vividness of that narrative, and the language-in-use for an experimental narrative (Spanish vs. English) were shown to determine a subject's high or low emotional identification with a central narrative character. (See Stolte and Fender, 2007, for methodological and empirical details.)

In summary, Chapters 1 and 2 have reviewed structural power-dependence as a general process theory. Also, these chapters have described an initial body of empirical research findings as well as important points of theoretical and methodological transition in the research program. We now turn to Part 2 of the book, (Chapters 3, 4 5, and 6). Each of these chapters reports a specific new study inspired by earlier questions, issues, and findings reported in studies published previously within the program. These chapters report new data gathered through the use of diverse research methods. As will be shown, these new studies draw from and build on the prior body of work anchored in the original line of research on structural power-dependence.

References

Ahmad, R., Nawaz, M.R., Ishaq, M.I., Khan, M.M., and Ashraf, H.A. (2023) Social exchange theory: Systematic review and future directions. *Front. Psychol.* 13:1015921. Doi: 0.3389/fpsyg.2022.1015921.

Bakan, D. (1966) The duality of human existence. Addison Wesley.

Bandura, A. (1977) Self-efficacy: toward a unifying theory of behavioral change. *Psychological Review* 84:191–95.

Berger, P. and Luckman, T. (1967) The social construction of reality. Knopf Doubleday.

Cooley, C.H. (1922) Human Nature and Social Order. Scribner.

Creelman, M. (1966) The experimental investigation of meaning. Springer.

Durkheim, E. (1964) The division of labor in society. (Translated by Simpson, G.) Collier-Macmillan.

Eckhoff, T. (1974) Justice: Its determinants in social interaction. Rotterdam University Press.

Emerson, R.M. (1962) Power-dependence relations. *American Sociological Review* 27:31–40.

Emerson, R.M. (1969) Operant psychology and exchange theory. In R.L. Burgess and D. Bushell (eds.) Behavioral Sociology, Columbia University Press.

Emerson, R.M. (1976) Social exchange theory. *Annual Review of Sociology* 2:335–62.

Emerson, R.M. (1981) Social exchange theory. In M. Rosenberg and R. Turner (eds.) Social Psychology: Sociological Perspectives, 30–65. Basic Books.

Emerson, R.M. (1972) Exchange theory: Parts I and II. In J. Berger, M. Eldritch, and B. Anderson (eds.) Sociological Theories in Progress, vol. 2, Houghton Mifflin.

Gecas, V. (1989) The social psychology of self-efficacy. *Annual Review of Sociology* 15:291–316.

Goffman, E. (1959) The Presentation of Self in Everyday Life. Knopf Doubleday.

Goffman, E. (1974). Frame Analysis. New York: Harper and Row.

Helgeson, V. (1994) Relation of agency and communion to well-being: Evidence and potential explanations. *Psychological Bulletin* 116, 3:412–428.

Hermans, H.J.M. (1996) Voicing the self: From information processing to dialogical interchange. *Psychological Bulletin* 119, 1:31–50.

Luria, A.R. (1981) Language and Cognition. In J.V. Wertsch (ed.) Language and Cognition, Wiley.

Markova, I. (1982) Paradigms, Thought, and Language. Wiley.

Markova, I. (2016) The Dialogical Mind. Cambridge University Press.

Mead, G.H. (1934) Mind, Self, and Society. University of Chicago Press.

Meeker, B. (1971) Decisions and exchange. *American Sociological Review* 36:485–95.

Mutran, E. and Reitzes, D. (1984) Inter-generational support activities and well-being among the elderly: A convergence of exchange and symbolic interaction perspectives. *American Sociological Review* 49:117–30.

Rammetveit, R. and Balkar, R.M. (1979) Studies of language, thought and verbal communication. Academic.

Saragovi, C., Koestner, R., & Di Dio, L. (1997) Agency, communion, and well-being: Extending Helgeson's (1994) model. *Journal of Personality and Social Psychology* 73, 3:593–609.

Seeman, M. (1959) On the meaning of alienation. *American Sociological Review*, 783–791.

Sewell, W.H. (1999) The concept(s) of culture. In V. Bonnell and L. Hunt (eds.) Beyond the Cultural Turn: New Directions in the Study of Society and Culture, University of California Press.

Singelmann, P. (1972) Exchange as symbolic interaction: Convergences between two theoretical perspectives. *American Sociological Review* 37, 4:414–424.

Stolte J.F. (1987a) The formation of justice norms. *American Sociological Review* 52, 6:774–784.

Stolte, J.F. (1987b) Legitimacy, justice, and productive exchange. In Karen S. Cook (ed.) Social Exchange Theory, 190–208, Sage.

Stolte, J.F. and Emerson, R. (1977) Structural inequality: Position and power in network structures. In R. Hamblin & J. Kunkel (eds.) Behavioral Theory in Sociology. Transaction Books.

Stolte, J.F. (1978a) Power structure and personal competence. *Journal of Social Psychology* 106:83–92.

Stolte, J.F. (2000) The value of socially extrinsic vs. intrinsic outcomes: An exploration of Americans from 1974–1994. *Social Behavior and Personality* 28, 4:387–392.

Stolte, J.F. and Fender, S. (2007) Framing social values: An experimental study of culture and cognition, Social Psychology Quarterly 70, 1:59–69.

Strauss, A. (1978) Negotiations: Varieties, Contexts, Processes, and Social Order. Jossey- Bass.

Tirolians, S., and Gaskell, G. (2011). The role of plurality and context in social values. *Journal for the Theory of Social Behavior*, 1–25.

Vygotsky, L. (1962) Thought and language, MIT.

Williams, R.M. and Albert, E.M. (1990) Values: The concept of values. *International Encyclopedia of the Social Sciences* 16:283–291.

Wolff, K. (1950) The Sociology of George Simmel. Free Press.

Zartman, I.W. (1977) Negotiation as a joint decision-making process. *Journal of Conflict Resolution* 21, 4:619–638.

Zartman, I.W. (2022) Justice in negotiating: How and where to find it and use it. *International Negotiation*, 1–29.

PART 2

Extending the Structural Power-Dependence Research Program: New Studies

∴

CHAPTER 3

Culture, Cognition, and Social Exchange: A Classic Case Study of Social Negotiation Network Dynamics

1 Culture and Cognition

1.1 *Setting the Agenda*

In sociology, Dimaggio (1997; 2002) argues that an understanding of culture, as experienced and enacted by the individual, needs to incorporate insights and findings from cognitive psychology. In his view, two facets of cognitive processing have special import: (a) automatic vs. controlled cognition, and (b) hot vs. cold cognition. Further, he argues, "Symbols, networks, and cognition" form a "crucial intersection" for analysis (Dimaggio, 1997:282), pointing "to a new, more complex understanding of the relationship between culture and social structure built upon careful integration of micro and macro, and of cognitive and material perspectives" (Dimaggio, 1997: 283). Cerulo (2002:3), building on Dimaggio's work in this area, urges the incorporation of a social neuroscience perspective in the study of culture and cognition. She notes, however, that sociologists should move beyond brain scan data to "locate and analyze cognition (neurological processing) in its sociocultural context."[1] More generally, Cerulo (2014, pp 1013) presses for the advancement of this important sociological project, suggesting a "two-step agenda:" first, "we should mine what we can from the abundant material provided by cognitive science" and second, "we should 'continue' those stories by applying sociological knowledge." The present study aims to contribute to the advancement of this significant sociological agenda.

---

1 Cerulo's position is roughly similar to that taken by behavioral and neuro-economists (Lowenstein, Scott, and Cohen, 2008; Gul and Pesendorfer, 2005). We should be measured in our embrace of "the new phrenology." While brain imaging data provide a more precise, more objective evidence base for understanding economic (and other social) behavior, such data merely intervene between objective social stimuli and objective social behavior in a larger causal sequence. The task remains to grasp the full causal sequence.

 | DOI:10.1163/9789004713918_004

1.2 *Key Issues Arising from Prior Cognitive Science*

In psychology, Markus and Kityama, (1991), with a focus on cross-cultural variations, distinguish individuals in eastern (e.g., Asian) cultures who construe the self in terms of social *interdependence* from individuals in western (e.g., American or European) cultures who construe the self in terms of *independence*. Proposing a more differentiated but quite congruent perspective, Fiske (1991) makes a case for the universality of four basic culture and cognition models: communal sharing, and equality matching (that seem to parallel the interdependent self), authority ranking, and market pricing (that seem to parallel the independent self).[2] (Also see: Stolte, 1992; Fiske, Kityama, Markus, and Nisbett, 1998).

Several questions arise. How do the automatic vs. controlled, hot vs. cold, and intrinsic-communal vs. extrinsic-agentic facets of culture and cognition work together in a socio-cultural perspective informed by social neuroscience? Can the oscillations between a lower, automatic, unconscious, non-verbal level and a higher, deliberative, conscious, verbal level of cultural cognition be clarified? Can the hot vs. cold dimension of processing that connects emotion and cultural cognition be spelled out? Can the intricate balance (or imbalance) of intrinsic-communal and extrinsic-agentic concerns in cultural cognition be better understood? Can social neuroscience add explanatory power to the study of cultural cognition? The present study explores these questions, aiming to build integrative connections among some key ideas.

As Cerulo has aptly argued, progress toward answering these sorts of questions requires consideration of individual cultural cognition explicitly within a social environmental context composed of other individuals, collectivities, and socio-cultural conditions. Three tasks must be accomplished: central

---

2 Other contributions to cultural psychology take a similar tack. Clark and Mills (1979; 1993; Clark and Finkel, 2005) distinguish instrumental exchange (e.g., business or market) relationships and social (e.g., family and friendship) relationships. Similarly, Abele and Wojciszke, (2007), build on Bakun's (1966) classic work, to contrast self-centered *agency* and other-centered *communion* as basic dimensions of culture and cognition giving structure to interpersonal perceptions and judgments between two actors. When agency has primacy, A and B are pushed apart. When communion has primacy, A and B are pulled together. Fiske's "communal sharing and equality matching," seem embodied within Bakun's concept of communion, while Fiske's "authority ranking and market pricing" seem encompassed within Bakun's notion of agency. Finally, Stolte and Fender, (2007) connect cultural psychology with social exchange theory, distinguishing an intrinsic social exchange relationship from an extrinsic social exchange relationship. In the former, A and B view one another as mutually valued ends, not instrumental means, and they mutually enjoy a close emotional bond with one another. In the latter, A and B view one another as instrumental means to other valued ends outside their relationship, and they stand at a greater emotional distance from one another.

features of social environmental context must be clearly demarcated; conditions shaping individual cultural cognition must be specified; the dynamic through which an individual, once shaped, effectively travels the socio-cultural landscape must be elucidated. The analysis below pursues these tasks.

The following discussion has four parts. First, Malinowski's classic study of the Kula exchange system is revisited and selectively summarized. Second, his study is thoroughly "re-imagined" in light of a structural power-dependence perspective on social negotiation networks (Stolte, 1983; 1987; 1988). Third, the processes through which individual cultural cognition is shaped within a social negotiation network setting are discussed. Fourth, the cultural cognitive dynamic through which an individual navigates the socio-cultural negotiation network is discussed.

Malinowski's ethnography is a useful starting point, because it provides a concrete, vivid glimpse of life and socio-cultural settings related to the issues investigated here. His iconic ethnographic research throws institutional culture and sub-institutional social exchange into bold relief. It offers lucid images and observations as raw material that can be theoretically re-worked to gain new insights about cultural cognition. Nevertheless, Malinowski's meta-theoretical commitments are problematic and limiting.

Falling squarely within the "functionalist" paradigm of ethnography (Sanday, 1979), his work must be criticized on the same general grounds as other social scientific work conducted exclusively within this paradigm. For example, in a classic and influential critique, Wrong (1961) notes that a strictly functionalist viewpoint over-emphasizes consensus, harmony, and integration among members of a socio-cultural setting, and it offers an "oversocialized" view of the individual. By pre-supposition, this viewpoint ignores the brute reality of social conflict. Such conflict, often entailing power and inequality, occurs pervasively, varies in intensity, and operates across the micro- to macro- span within and between human actors.

To be clear, however, the functionalist perspective, should not be judged as entirely incorrect or lacking theoretical value. There are, of course, both consensual-integrating and conflict-separating forces operating across most, if not all, social relationships. As elaborated in the discussion of mixed-motive interactions below, the negotiation network framework offers theoretical strengths for capturing both consensus and conflict in social life.

We turn next, then, to a brief sketch of the Kula ring.

2 Old but Still Relevant Ethnographic Findings: Malinowski, 1920

The focus here is on a narrow but important slice of Bronislaw Malinowski's enduring work. Drawing from an early article (Malinowski, 1920), we outline key features of the socio-cultural life and setting of the trading peoples who inhabited the archipelagoes of New Guinea. His report describes "a special system of trade," the "Kula," which, he noted, says something interesting and important about both "primitive economics" and "native mentality" (Malinowski, 1920:97). As Malinowski forcefully argues, there is a fundamental link between the ecology of human (economic and social) exchange and cultural cognition.

A few points from Malinowski's concrete description can be selected for emphasis to create a simpler, if more abstract, conceptualization. Imagine two people. Chief S leads the island people of Sinaketa. A long distance away, across rough, high, dangerous seas, Chief D heads the island people of Dobu. Suppose the two chiefs and their respective bands of followers have established a longitudinal exchange relationship. At the customary time in a given season, S and her/his fellow traders prepare a sea-worthy canoe with great care, in strict conformity with appropriate magical activities. They brave rough waters, sailing to D's island. After being welcomed, at the prescribed time, S offers an initiating Kula article, a decorative armshell, to D, who accepts with delight. After appropriate time has passed, D offers a return Kula article, an ornamental necklace, to S, who likewise accepts it with pleasure. This exchange of articles is the social symbolic core of the Kula exchange system. The Kula institution, followed regularly for many generations, forms a crucial cultural boundary around a diverse set of communities, knitting together a far-flung set of disparate island peoples. Malinowski was deeply impressed by the "enormous geographical extent of the trading system" (Malinowski, 1920:97) whose intricate pattern he traced, documented, and studied in depth.

One reason the Kula exchange system fascinated Malinowski is that it stood in bold contrast to ordinary economic exchange, which regularly occurred right alongside it. The island traders continuously transmitted to one another such "highly useful utilities" as "canoes or pottery ... dried fish or yams" (Malinowski, 1920: 97). An objective observer (Malinowski) could see these material articles of ordinary economic exchange were indispensable for biological survival, health, and the general quality of island life. Ironically and interestingly, however, the traders themselves were not particularly excited about the outcomes of such "subsidiary exchange" (Malinowski, 1920:97). Rather, economic outcomes and "common (economic) barter" were viewed as mundane, routine objects and events, nothing to get excited about. Ordinary economic exchange was viewed as a pedestrian, if necessary, activity, hardly worth much attention or effort. Instead, the island traders were consumed by, and energetically devoted to, attaining better, finer, armshells and necklaces, articles "of high value but of no real use" (Malinowski, 1920:97). Obtaining an especially fine armshell or necklace stirred considerable talk among members of the surrounding community. A trader's positive reputation, social prestige, about which a trader cared a lot, was clearly contingent on the longitudinal acquisition of Kula outcomes of higher and higher value.

A substantial corpus of mystical knowledge and practice had evolved around the Kula. Traders would often conduct magic rites and speak magic spells. If Chief S needed potency in dealing with Chief D, so that D would more likely grant her/him a highly valuable armshell, S would cast a magic spell "to shake the mountain" (Malinowski, 1920: 104). The purpose was to generate awe in D, yet keep D from getting so angry as to leave the trading relationship. A Kula transaction was delicate. It required just the right "touch." Magical rites and incantations were used to facilitate the entire Kula enterprise, from building a safe, ocean-worthy canoe, to warding off dangers during travel, through manipulating opposing traders during Kula transactions. Also, an elaborate mythology had evolved across the generations to augment the value of Kula exchange. Legends regarding prior sailings to other islands, difficulties encountered, treasures obtained, were created and passed on through stories. "In myths, in traditional legends, in real stories and in songs, Kula expeditions were and are described and praised and there is a definite complex of Kula tradition and mythology" (Malinowski, 1920: 103).

The Kula was a firmly institutionalized and stable form of social symbolic exchange. It was a tightly regulated system of social interaction based on long-held and widely accepted cultural norms. Presenting an initial article (an armshell), presenting a return article (a necklace), were features of exchange guided by mutually held cultural expectations, supported by most island inhabitants. To violate a Kula expectation did not bring a formally administered coercive sanction. A deviant was not arrested, placed in shackles, and/or beaten. But a Kula violation did bring probable and serious social disapprobation, and, was thereby effectively suppressed by the community. In regard to Kula trading, most islanders did what they were supposed to do most of the time.

Cultural rules dictated the direction in which a given Kula article could "travel" through exchange. An armshell always travelled a counter-clockwise route, and a necklace always travelled a clock-wise route through the New Guinea island chain. Also, the rules commanded an article (armshell or necklace) not be "possessed" for long, but rather be put back into circulation quite soon. Ironically, a trader, skillfully maneuvering to obtain an especially valuable article (of fine size, color, artistic beauty), was strictly obliged, and rather soon (exact period of time not specified), to pass it on in a subsequent transaction. Beyond an appropriate period of time, keeping and displaying an article, in a vigorous attempt to magnify one's own social prestige, was proscribed. A Kula article obtained was "a temporary possession ... (kept) in trust for a time" (Malinowski, 1920: 100). In Malinowski's words (1920:100), "The Kula involves the elements of trust and of a sort of commercial honour".

Indeed, in Malinowski's functionalist paradigm, trust and honor were pervasive and crucial for sustaining the overall quality of social and economic life among the island traders. They required a trustworthy and honorable world in order to be willing to commence frightening, dangerous journeys by boat to distant islands for Kula exchange and material trade. They wanted considerable assurance in advance they would be met as traders, not enemies, when they arrived. They needed basic assistance and safety as they ventured to faraway territories ruled by strangers. They had to know with considerable certainty that they would be housed, fed, and protected from harm when they arrived.

It is noteworthy, then, that this culturally prescribed bond of basic trust and honor upon which Malinowski dwells, existed right alongside inherent competition and social friction that he himself also clearly documented between island traders. First, there was "common barter" entailed in "subsidiary (material-economic) exchange." Issues of mutual contention might include small or large questions: How big a canoe will Chief S give in exchange for how many pots and yams returned by Chief D? Second, there was the mutual desire to get Kula articles of higher and higher social prestige value across time, despite the obvious scarcity of such beautiful articles. What would Chief S be prepared to offer as additional (material) incentives to Chief D to persuade D to provide an especially elegant and beautiful necklace as a part of the Kula symbolic exchange itself? Such questions highlight the natural, inevitable conflicts of interest that characterized relations among the island traders, in parallel with their collective cooperative interests, and in addition to the socially binding qualities of trust and honor. As Malinowski (1920: 100) explicitly noted: "This, of course, does not completely exclude many squabbles, deep resentments and even feuds over real or imaginary grievances in the Kula exchange."

3 "Re-imagining" the Kula as a Social Negotiation Network

In what follows, Malinowski's observations and interpretations are "re-construed" in light of ideas drawn selectively from prior work (Stolte and Emerson, 1977; Stolte, 1983; 1987;1988) centered on power-dependence (Emerson, 1962) in structures of social exchange (Emerson, 1969;1972;1981). The prior work deals with negotiated transactions and benefit-outcomes occurring across time among individuals located in exchange relations, exchange networks, and productive exchange groups. This line of work is but one tributary flowing from the widely influential theory of structural exchange originated by Richard M. Emerson (1969; 1972; 1976; 1981), whose brilliant contributions remain far under-appreciated in sociology today.

3.1 *Foundations: Structural Power-Dependence and Exchange*

Let us return to and incorporate basic ideas introduced in Part I above as they relate to the present context. For the moment, consider only T1 and T2 in Illustration 7 below. Suppose the line between these actors represents an established, longitudinal social exchange relationship between island trader T1 (perhaps Chief S described above) and island trader T2 (perhaps Chief D described above). This relationship entails a series of transactions. According to established Kula custom, in each such transaction, T1 provides a necklace, while T2 provides an armshell. T2 values necklaces obtained from T1, and T1 values armshells obtained from T2.[3] The common value obtained by both T1

3 We follow Emerson (1969; 1972; 1981) in assuming that *anything* that enters social exchange as a resource or benefit (a Kula article—armshell or necklace) has value. Each party to an exchange relation is "motivationally invested" in obtaining what the other party can provide. For a given actor, resources/benefits lie in different value domains. An interesting question centers on the relative value of different domains. (See Stolte, 2000) In the present context, T1 might value both Kula armshells as a source of social prestige as well as regular drinks of cool, fresh water. Whether an armshell or a drink of water has relatively greater value to this island trader at a given time, will depend on which domain is currently most *uncertain*. If fresh water is readily available, easily and routinely obtained, whenever the need for water arises, the *felt need for water* is very low and the trader will place low value on a drink of water compared to an armshell worth social prestige whose acquisition may have been quite uncertain. Assuming that getting sufficient water is not problematic, Kula traders throughout the island society might well have channeled considerably more behavioral energy toward the attainment of Kula articles than water. Water (along with canoes, yams, pots, or any other material or symbolic benefit-outcomes) might be relegated down a hierarchy of value to relatively mundane, uninspiring "subsidiary exchange." Malinowski's observations described above, as well as ethnographic data collected by Sahlins (2000), at a much later time in a different societal context, are consistent with this behavioral theory that causally links uncertainty and value. Sahlins describes the "original affluent society," a band

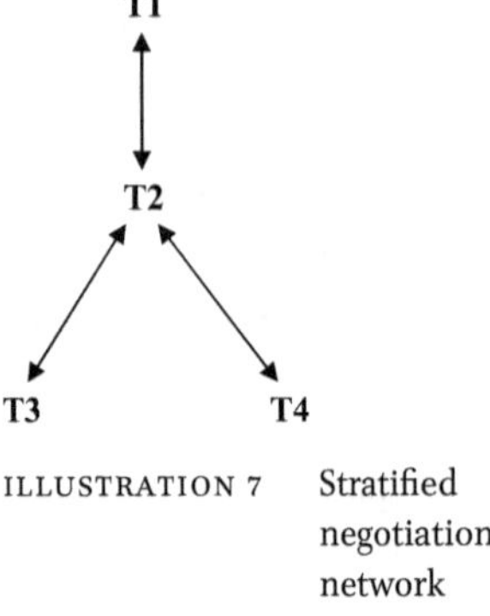

ILLUSTRATION 7 Stratified negotiation network

and T2 through Kula transactions is island- society-wide social prestige (notoriety, positive social recognition). The finer and more beautiful an article a given trader obtains, the more prestige a trader commands from other islanders. But, following Malinowski's observations, Kula articles, whether armshells or necklaces, vary substantially in their social prestige value. Some finely crafted and beautiful articles are worth relatively high social prestige in the community. Other not so finely crafted rather plain articles are worth relatively low prestige. We assume that the finer, more artistic, more unique the article, the rarer (and scarcer) it will be. Consequently, prestige was a scarce benefit-outcome, an uncertain benefit-outcome. It seems likely that such prestige was therefore of relatively high value though of "no real utility."

Suppose T1 and T2 both place relatively *high and equal value* on social prestige. As strongly suggested by Malinowski's evidence, island traders such as T1 and T2 are motivated to "drive hard bargains," using whatever tactics and cultural tools they can muster, energetically seeking to obtain Kula articles that are as beautiful and prestigious as the circumstances permit. As Malinowski tells us, a given trader might well add an additional material resource proffer (offer to throw in a canoe plus a sack of yams) to supplement the symbolic Kula transaction. Or, an islander might employ special preparatory magic rites (attempt "to shake the mountain"), in a vigorous self-serving effort to achieve the very best possible Kula outcome. We assume that any circumstance that would stand in the way of a given islander obtaining higher rather than lower

of nomadic hunters/gatherers who enjoyed considerable leisure, plenty of calories, and a relative life of ease because, evidently, what they needed biologically from their environment, could be obtained readily (with little uncertainty) through an adaptive life- style of ready and frequent nomadic travel to alternative ecological settings where needed resources were available in profusion for ready consumption.

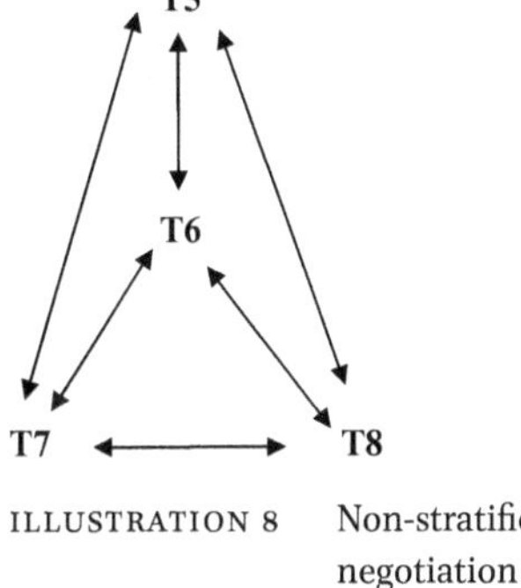

ILLUSTRATION 8 Non-stratified negotiation network

T9------T10------T11------T12

ILLUSTRATION 9 Productive exchange system (group or division of labor)

Kula prestige will be resisted. Any circumstance that puts T1's gains in Kula prestige at odds with T2's gains in Kula prestige (and vice versa), will create mutual resistance between them.

Whenever an exchange relationship between two parties, for example T1 and T2, is characterized by mutual resistance, social power dynamics are activated. Following Emerson (1962), the power of T1 over T2 is equal to the amount of resistance in T2 that can potentially be overcome by T1 (and vice versa). Further, T1's power is determined by T2's dependence upon T1 for benefit-outcomes sought by T2 (and vice versa). The greater T2's dependence, the greater T1's power (and vice versa). From T1's and/or T2's perspective, dependence upon the other is, in turn, set by two variables: the more highly either actor *values* benefit-outcomes provided by the other, the greater that actor's dependence on the other; also, the more *available* benefit-outcomes are outside the relationship from alternative sources (e.g., other island traders), the lower T1's dependence on T2 or (vice versa).

Power-dependence in the Kula exchange relation between T1 and T2 might, theoretically, be equal or unequal. The mutual value and availability factors might be situationally arranged such that T1 and T2 are equally dependent upon one another, a circumstance granting each island trader equal power over the other in the face of mutual resistance. Or the two underlying determinants of power-dependence might be situationally arranged so that one islander is less dependent and the other more dependent. Consequently, one trader might have relatively greater power within the Kula exchange relation than the other.

Expanding these points, power-dependence theory asserts that where one actor (T2) is less dependent upon another actor (T1), T2 enjoys a power advantage in the exchange relationship. A power advantage (in the theory's inexorable logic) will tend to be used across a longitudinal series of exchange transactions. Such power use will lead to an increase in the value of benefit-outcomes enjoyed by the power-advantaged actor without an increase (indeed, often with a relative decrease) in the value of benefit-outcomes obtained by the power- disadvantaged actor across time. If T1 and T2 happen to have equal power-dependence, neither trader has an advantage, mutual power will be balanced, and no power will be used in the exchange process. Under this circumstance, Kula transactions are likely to entail armshell- for-necklace transactions entailing the mutual distribution of equal levels of social prestige across time. That is, because power-dependence is balanced between T1 and T2, the benefit- outcomes of exchange transactions will be balanced and equal. However, if either island trader has a power-advantage, that advantage will tend to be used longitudinally across transactions.[4] T1 and/or T2 may or may not have clear knowledge about the wider circumstances bearing upon Kula transactions, but regardless of what these two island traders know (and know accurately), when "push comes to shove," when each island trader works enthusiastically to "drive a hard bargain" in an effort to achieve the very best possible armshell (or necklace) benefit-outcome possible (i.e., get the most social prestige possible), the islander with a power-dependence *advantage* will tend to benefit relatively more than the islander with a power-dependence *disadvantage* across the longitudinal series of exchange transactions. That is to say, power-dependence disparities in Kula exchange relations are likely to lead to benefit-outcome *stratification* among islanders across time. (Incidentally, and apropos of this

4 The prediction that power advantage will be used is a "structural" principle, and no explicit awareness, cognition, or shared social knowledge on the part of either Kula trader about the overall exchange situation is *presumed* (see Stolte, 1983, for an expanded discussion). On the other hand, awareness, cognition and shared social knowledge at some level is not ruled out by this principle. Indeed, as noted earlier, a major goal of Stolte's (1987) social negotiation network approach and the present study is to explicitly incorporate and explore and the significance of such awareness, cognition, and shared social knowledge (symbolic interaction, more generally).

point, Malinowski clearly documents the distinction between Chiefs and commoners in his ethnography.)[5]

From the power-dependence theory point of view, stratification among island traders in social prestige is *structurally* determined. Consider Illustration 7. In this Kula structure, T2 occupies a relatively advantaged *position* in the negotiation network, by virtue of the *"availability"* determinant of dependence (and thus power), as described above (also see Stolte and Emerson, 1977). Across a series of transactions, T2 is likely to obtain increasingly favorable Kula benefit-outcomes. Conversely, T1 is unlikely to obtain such increasingly favorable Kula outcomes. Theoretically, that is to say, T2 has a position-based power-dependence advantage relative to T1 in the Kula social negotiation network. Put simply, T2 enjoys a relative abundance of alternative transaction sources (other potential Kula trading partners) with whom that trader can choose to exchange Kula articles, should resistance be encountered.[6] Theoretically, the position-based power advantage enjoyed by T2 over T1 will gradually be "used" across a series of transactions. Across time, the net Kula benefit-outcomes in social prestige value enjoyed by T2 will substantially exceed those enjoyed by T1.

Now consider the important contrast between Illustrations 7 and 8. The first illustration is an *open* exchange network configured such that position-based

---

5 Malinowski notes the general cultural expectation that one island trader provide a Kula article that is of equivalent value to the Kula article obtained from another island trader in a given transaction. However, he also notes that on certain occasions (the frequency is left unspecified) a given trader is unable to do this, and is culturally expected to attempt to rectify this imbalance in subsequent transactions if possible. Also, Malinowski discusses how traders attempt to influence the quality of articles obtained in trade, for example, by employing magic incantations and rites to "shake the mountain," as described above. Thus, one is left with the strong impression that Kula trades might well involve variation in the quality of outcomes between traders. In other words, Kula transactions can, at least sometimes (perhaps more frequently than Malinowski's functional approach might suggest), lead to social prestige benefit-outcomes to the advantage of one trader over another. That is, the operation of power-dependence in Kula exchange can produce a social stratification of prestige among island traders, with some enjoying higher and others settling for lower levels of island prestige.

6 The exchange structural disparity shown in Illustration 3.1 operates on two levels. At a relatively more micro-social level, one can focus on the position-within-the network, noting that T2's *position-based* power-dependence is greater than T1's (or T3's or T4's). Or at a relatively more *macro-social* level one can focus on the network as a whole, looking at the contrast between Illustrations 3.1 and 3.2. As discussed earlier, Stolte (1988) provides measures of both positional and network-wide power disparities as well as experimental data demonstrating the impact of such exchange structural power disparities on benefit-outcome stratification among subjects in laboratory experimental social exchange networks.

power-dependence is unequal in favor of T2 relative to T1, T3, and T4 within that structure. By contrast, Illustration 8 is a completely *closed* social exchange network, where every trader is directly connected in Kula exchange with every other trader, every trader has an equal number of trading partners (i.e., "availability" is equal), and position-based power-dependence is equally distributed. As experimental research has shown (Stolte and Emerson, 1977), a structure like the one drawn in Illustration 8 can be identified as a "closed social circle," which, by virtue of the "availability" determinant of relative dependence (and therefore power), allocates equal power-dependence to every actor in the network. In the present context, each island trader in Illustration 8 enjoys a level of power-dependence equal to the level enjoyed by every other island trader in that structure. Therefore, across a series of exchange transactions (Kula trades), all island traders are predicted to obtain equal levels of Kula benefit-outcomes and social prestige.

Now consider the contrast between Illustrations 7 and 8, on the one hand, and Illustration 9, on the other hand. This contrast is between exchange networks with varying distributions of power-dependence, unequal and equal, respectively (Illustrations 7 and 8), and an "incorporated" productive exchange system, or "collective actor" (Illustration 9). Again drawing inspiration from Malinowski, suppose a given island Chief mobilizes a set of commoners/followers on a given island to prepare for and launch a major Kula trade expedition to a distant island across rough, dangerous waters. Such an expedition is a *collective (group) enterprise*. No one trader will get a benefit-outcome, unless all get benefit-outcomes. To effectively mount such an expedition, the traders will need to divide the relevant labor somehow. Each trader will need to undertake a portion of the work to be accomplished, perhaps locating and obtaining the best wood, helping to carve the wood into an ocean-worthy craft, participating enthusiastically in the appropriate and prescribed magic rituals surrounding such an expedition. Then, leaving together as a united, solidary "collective actor" (organized group) (Emerson, 1972; Stolte, 1987), the traders must jointly venture forth across a threatening ocean and return safely with a store of Kula articles promising a relatively large level of aggregate social prestige.[7]

Note that any relationship entailing negotiated social exchange, whether embedded within an *open*, power-unequal/stratified exchange network depicted in Illustration 7, a *closed*, power-equal/non-stratified exchange network shown in Illustration 8, or a productive exchange system displayed in

7 See Emerson 1972; 1981; Barth, 1966; Stolte, 1987 for related discussions of "productive exchange systems" or "incorporated groups" as distinctive social exchange structures that differ fundamentally from social exchange networks.

Illustration 9, must be seen as a *mixed-motive relationship*. Each such relationship will always entail both a cooperative/integrative and a competitive/distributive interest, lying below the surface that may or may not become explicit. However, which "side" of the relationship becomes relatively more salient in a given instance is an open empirical question. Such salience will depend on the surrounding exchange structural configuration and the dynamic longitudinal process of exchange through which benefit-outcomes are determined and distributed. Theoretically, more competition is expected to occur in a stratified structure such as Illustration 7: T1, T3, and T4 will spend relatively more time and behavioral energy competing with one another to make trades with T2. T2 will receive many offers and is in a position to choose the most valuable outcome from any trade offered. By contrast, less competition is expected in Illustration 8: T5, T6, T7, and T8 are structural equals, no power advantage is enjoyed by any trader, and trades will lead to an equal distribution of Kula social prestige outcomes for traders across a series of transactions. Finally, even less competition, as well as more explicit cooperation, is expected in a productive exchange system, as depicted in Illustration 9. Although each relationship between a trader and the collective actor continues to be mixed-motive in nature, the salience of the cooperative/integrative side will tend to exceed the salience of the competitive/distributive side in a unified collective actor. Working hard together in energetic preparations for and conduct of a Kula-seeking sea voyage, the traders are expected to exhibit a relatively high level of "social solidarity" or "group cohesiveness." Such a state is likely to remain in effect as long as members remain united in pursuit of the collective outcome. During this time, the cooperative/integrative dimension of the relationship between each trader and the group at large is likely to be relatively more salient. After the traders have returned home with a new store of valued Kula articles, however, as the current collective enterprise comes to an end and the open or closed exchange network becomes re-established, the salience of the other side of the mixed-motive relationship is expected to increase: Kula prestige must now be distributed. Who gets relatively more, and who gets relatively less social prestige? Hence, the integrative/cooperative side of the mixed motive relationship will become quiescent and the competitive/distributive side of each relationship will again gain prominence. Variation in structural exchange circumstances leads to variation in the salience of the two sides of the mixed-motive relationship within a social negotiation network.

4 Social Negotiation Networks and the Emergence of Culture: From Sub-institutional to Institutional Exchange

Stolte (1983; 1987) argues that we can and should introduce theoretical ideas explicitly addressing issues of awareness, cognition, and shared social knowledge (culture) into the power-dependence/structural exchange framework. One key idea is *social negotiation,* an exchange-relevant form of interpersonal communication, through which two parties to a social exchange relationship come to agreements across the series of transactions. For example, T1 and T2 engage in such communication as they mutually settle on a longitudinal set of agreements to mutually transmit Kula articles, armshells for necklaces.[8]

Based on the social negotiation process, a cultural institution, such as the Kula trading system (or any other cultural arrangement) can be understood to evolve within an underlying structure power-dependence/social exchange (Stolte, 1987).

Imagine an earlier time, perhaps generations earlier, among the Island peoples of New Guinea, prior to the time of the Kula. Suppose that getting sufficient material resources (e.g., canoes, yams, pots, fish, etc.) was far more pressing at this earlier historical time than when Malinowski studied the islanders in 1920. Presume that the island peoples began trading economic, not symbolic, goods and services in order to cope with such material scarcity.

Perhaps in that earlier time, exchange/trading relationships assumed structural forms like those shown in Illustration 7. But at that time, assume that only "underlying exigencies of structural exchange, mutual resource dependence, and the dynamics of power" existed (Stolte, 1987: 777). Power-dependence/structural exchange theory *per se* limits its focus exclusively to such underlying exigencies of exchange. As noted earlier, that theory is "formulated entirely in objective, behavioral, cognition-free terms" and it "excludes perceptions, expectations, meanings, understandings" from its purview (Stolte, 1987: 777). However, in order to build an adequate account of the way a cultural institution such as the Kula (or any other cultural institution) evolves within and

8 As noted earlier, the negotiation network approach (also see Stolte, 1990) incorporates elements of symbolic interaction theory into Emerson's structural social exchange theory. However, we contend that traditional symbolic interaction theory dwells too much on the "higher order verbal/logical" (deliberative) facets of cognition, often failing to address crucial lower-order, non-verbal, non-logical, "automatic" facets of cognition. The present monograph aims to deal more explicitly with the full range of the dual cognitive processing that occurs within social negotiation as a form of communication. Also see Paivio (2007) for a systematic treatment of the intricate interrelationship of verbal and non-verbal capacities in the evolution of the human mind.

from such sub-institutional exchange structures and dynamics, we must introduce additional theoretical concepts and principles.

These additional concepts/principles can be found in a synthesis of several ideas focused on the interplay of the symbolic/verbal and non-symbolic/non-verbal processing capacities of the human animal (Baldwin and Baldwin, 1978; Mead, 1934; Vygotsky, 1962; Paivio, 2007). Especially pertinent is a distinction between two kinds of knowledge, *tacit vs. explicit* (Baldwin and Baldwin, 1978). Tacit knowledge is formed through a person's direct encounters with immediate environmental "contingencies." Suppose in ancient pre-Kula times, traders T1 and T2 discover they can arrive at a mutually beneficial trade of a fine canoe for needed yams, fish, and pots. The subjective knowledge each trader acquires from this underlying material exchange is tacit.[9] Such knowledge is "private and rich in emotional meaning" (Stolte, 1987: 777). Such knowledge is concrete and situational. But, we assume, the two traders, as well as the other inhabitants of the New Guinea islands, are also able to use language for communication. Such symbolic/verbal capacity permits them to translate merely individual, concrete, tacit knowledge into more abstract, public, shared knowledge. The verbal/symbolic capacity of the traders permits them to form explicit "social and collective meaning agreements" which are essential to the formation of any cultural institution. There is an important change in the evolution from tacit to explicit knowledge: "to know the objective world explicitly is to grasp and react to it in terms of verbal and non-verbal signs, the meanings of which are established in human communication" (Stolte, 1987: 777).

In sum, meaning agreements (mutual awareness, social cognition, shared social knowledge) arise interpersonally through social negotiation, as that process attends the exchange of benefit-outcomes. Across a span of time, meaning agreements are shaped and re- shaped. They become more or less widely shared. These meaning agreements come to cover many or most facets of social and material life.[10]

9 "Tacit" knowledge is very close in meaning to what contemporary dual process theorists call "intuitive" (Haidt, 2001; Evans, 2008). Baldwin and Baldwin (1978) advanced the distinction between tacit and explicit well prior to the contemporary dual-process distinction between "automatic" and "controlled/deliberative".

10 Stolte (1987) limited his focus to the way "justice norms" (equality, equity, need, status) are formed through social negotiation under varying conditions of structural power-dependence. But the current analysis intends to expand the scope of such socially negotiated meaning agreements to virtually any aspect of the social life of a people, small or large. Thus, we aim to argue here that the entire Kula trading system, as a cultural institution, was formed gradually through this sort of dynamic process.

As cultural meaning agreements form and re-form through social negotiation among actors in exchange relations, exchange networks, and productive exchange systems, boundaries around "collective actors" are formed and re-formed. Two actors, T1 and T2, might come to mutually form an "interpersonal meaning agreement," a shared body of social knowledge at the social dyad-level. But such social knowledge does not itself constitute a cultural institution. At a minimum, such an institution requires a social triad, as this point was classically formulated by Simmel (Wolf, 1950). Or as Stolte (1987: 779) puts it, drawing from the classic statement by Simmel, shared social knowledge does not qualify as a cultural norm until "it is 'super-individual' in its objective, exterior, facticity." Within the present example, before a cultural institution can be said to exist, T1 would need to be confronted, at a minimum, by a unified "collective actor" composed of T2 and T3 acting together under one unified normative policy, or better, by all the other actors in the trading network, including T4. A cultural institution presupposes that each individual subject to its influence is confronted by a collectivity "acting in concert," standing above any given member of the collectivity, uniformly sanctioning obedience to its shared expectations. A "collective actor" can be construed as a powerful social coalition, upon which each member is dependent for valuable benefit-outcomes (Stolte, 1987). When culturally instituted, such a collectivity has the power (legitimate authority) to sanction any member located inside its boundaries. Significant deviation from cultural expectations will lead to significant sanctions. Each member standing within the cultural boundary of an instituted collective actor "understands" at some level[11] that action in conformity with the collectively agreed cultural norms will bring significant positive benefit-outcomes, while violation of the cultural norm(s) agreed to by the collective actor will fetch substantial losses of such outcomes.

Gradually, we imagine, the traders of the New Guniea islands came to conquer the practical issues of material survival, importantly through widening material exchange/trading (e.g., canoes for pots and foodstuffs) across the islands. Perhaps, as Sahlins (2000) argues, the New Guinea traders gradually established a relatively "affluent society." If so, they gradually would have discovered that meeting material needs became quite certain and routine, allowing time and energy for other facets of social life. It might well have been the case that these island peoples began to view "subsidiary (material) exchange" as a relatively routine, pedestrian, uninteresting, if necessary, task

11 The level of understanding might vary between two poles: a lower "automatic/unconscious" and a higher "conscious/controlled/deliberative" level.

to be regularly undertaken. At such a point, these island peoples might well have become increasingly excited about objects of increasing "value, but of no real use." Perhaps the basic idea of the Kula was begun. From there, the Kula symbolic social exchange system, with its promise of reputation and social prestige in the community, might have evolved further. New Kula rules, rituals, mythology, magic might have been socially negotiated. Perhaps the cultural inventions surrounding Kula were gradually but steadily embellished, as they were passed across the generations from the elders to youth through stories, legends, etc.[12]

5 Cultural Cognition in Social Negotiation Networks

In light of the background provided above, we now explore two sets of issues. First, we consider how an individual is culturally shaped within a negotiation network setting. Second, we examine how, once shaped, an individual navigates the practical micro-terrain of the negotiation network. Again, the re-imagined Kula inspires hypothetical concrete illustrations.

5.1 *Shaping Cultural Cognition*

Suppose traversing a life-course, from birth to death, through the island society described by Malinowski, gave cultural shape to the way islanders thought, felt, and acted, individually, relationally, and collectively. Assume that a member of the overall island culture is significantly shaped within varying, quite distinct *sub-cultures*. Also assume that each sub-cultural setting is a "collective actor," having a well-defined socio-cultural boundary based on a shared meaning agreement. Thus, each islander located within that boundary is confronted by a "super-individual," unified coalition, mobilized and ready to sanction obedience to its shared cultural expectations. We contend two kinds of sub-cultural settings have general significance in composing the overall culture of a negotiation network. The basic features of these two crucial settings are sketched below.

12 Within the structural power-dependence social negotiation network approach, the two levels, sub-institutional and cultural institutional, are always there. Further, we argue, in respect to the cultural cognition happening within the individual there will always be a dynamic interplay between the implicit/tacit meanings of concrete situational contingencies and the explicit meanings evidently shared and discussed by the members of the bounded, surrounding "collective actor" that enter discourse about what is taken as shared and public knowledge.

5.2 *Cultural Content: Two Basic Value Domains*

A first category of sub-cultural setting is organized around the achievement of *intrinsic-communal* benefit-outcomes. Collective actors structured in variations of productive exchange, as depicted in Illustration 9, provide an underlying model for such settings. At the most basic level, family and friendship groups illustrate this category of setting. Members of these groups usually have intimate, emotionally significant attachments to one another. Also within this first category of sub-cultural setting are various other groups based on productive exchange. Members of these other groups form emotional bonds of mutual identification, which, while not typically as strong or significant as family or friendship bonds, can sometimes become very strong and significant. Examples might include collaborative work groups, political groups, ethnic groups, racial groups, gender groups, ideology groups, and others. Intrinsic-communal settings are places (culturally bounded collective actors) where relatively high value is placed on self-subordination and self-sacrifice in the service of a (n) individual or collective "other(s)." As Stolte and Fender (2007) note, each party to a transaction within such a sub-cultural setting views the other party as an *end* rather than a *means*. Or, in a way, the other party *is* the benefit-outcome to be achieved. It is within such sub-cultural settings that empathy, sympathy, altruism, patriotism, camaraderie and similar social emotions are typically experienced (Hiadt, 2001; Batson, 1987).

A second category of sub-cultural setting is organized around the acquisition of *extrinsic-agentic* benefit-outcomes. Bounded collective actors with structures like Illustrations 7and 8 constitute this kind of setting. Malinowski's subsidiary (material) exchange and Kula symbolic exchange systems provide an apt illustration. Generally, individuals located within this kind of sub-cultural setting do not have strong, close emotional attachments to one another. Relatively high value is placed on extrinsic-agentic benefit-outcomes. Self-service and self-promotion by each individual are strongly encouraged. In Stolte and Fender's (2007) terms, each party to a transaction in this kind of setting views the other mainly as an *instrumental means* to benefit-outcomes deriving from outside the relationship. T1 and T2 view one another primarily as a useful means to Kula-borne social prestige, not as a dear old friend, going way back, sharing a significant history of mutual affection. Depending on one's relative success in this sort of setting, one may feel the ecstasy of triumph or humiliation of defeat, pleasure of success or shame of failure, glow of prominence or gloom of insignificance, warmth of pride or cold of disgrace.[13]

13 Within the social negotiation network perspective, an individual's relative success in an extrinsic-agentic setting, will be determined largely by that individual's relative positional

Assume that ordinarily (typically, on average) an individual islander is shaped to place value on *both kinds of benefit-outcomes*, intrinsic-communal and extrinsic-agentic.[14] Also assume, however, that individual differences in cultural shaping are probable. Consider individuals A, B, and C. Actor A might be culturally shaped to place approximately equal value on both intrinsic-communal and extrinsic-agentic benefit-outcomes. Actor B might be shaped to value intrinsic-communal outcomes substantially more than extrinsic-agentic outcomes. Actor C might be shaped to value extrinsic-agentic outcomes significantly more than intrinsic-communal outcomes. As noted below, studying the implications of these sorts of individual differences would be a worthwhile goal for future empirical research.

5.3 *The Shaping Process*

Imagine that an individual islander is formed longitudinally across the life-course in the context of varying sub-cultural settings, under the influence of varying collective actors. We contend that the two value-domains and sub-cultural settings described above are especially basic in the cultural shaping of the individual. Undoubtedly, cultural shaping is complex, probably entailing several connected processes. Based on prior theory and research, the following components of cultural shaping are likely to be most central.

"Externalization" is probably one important part of the cultural shaping process. Fiske (1991) captures this component well (also see Stolte, 1992; and Fiske, Kityama, Nesbitt, 1998). Basically, the individual is born with a biologically given set of potentialities, propensities, present at birth, which unfold sequentially across a series of developmental stages.[15] These qualities are "neurologically pre-wired." Each quality is an inherent "readiness" for or receptivity to varying kinds of external environmental stimulation. In Fiske's language, each quality is an inherent (perhaps universal) readiness to acquire each one of a varying set of cultural models: "communal sharing (CS)," "equality matching (EM)," "authority ranking (AR)," or "market pricing (MP)." Each cultural model can be thought of as a distinct "logic of action," in Dimaggio's (1997) sense. The

power-dependence. For a discussion of some related social psychological issues see Stolte (1983) on the "legitimation of structural inequality".

14 We follow Stolte and Fender (2007) here, contrasting the present analysis with the analysis advanced by Markus and Kityama (1991). The latter authors emphasize cross-cultural variations in selves (interdependent vs. independent). We emphasize multiple aspects of a self (intrinsic-communal vs. extrinsic-agentic) that might operate at different times in different (varying sub-cultural) situations within a single overall culture.

15 Of course, classic contributions by Piaget (1958) and Kohlberg (1969) laid important groundwork for Fiske's more recent cultural model externalization approach.

models can be collapsed into two categories corresponding quite closely to the two value domains, two sub-cultural settings, described above. An inherent neurological readiness to acquire CS and EM renders an individual sensitive to the give-and-take (social negotiation) with members of an intrinsic-communal setting. In contrast, a pre-wired neurological propensity to externalize AR and MP predisposes an individual to be sensitive to the exchange transactions occurring among members of an extrinsic-agentic setting.

"Socialization," is likely to be a second important component of the cultural shaping process, and it is neatly conveyed by Bandura's (1986) social learning framework. His approach presupposes basic Skinnerian mechanisms of operant conditioning (strengthening a tendency to behave in a given way through reinforcement, weakening a tendency to behave in a given way through punishment, and establishing "cues" through associative conditioning that set the situational occasion for behaving or not behaving in a given way). But Bandura's social learning approach develops a far richer and more subtle set of learning capacities within the individual than Skinner's simplistic, mechanistic operant conditioning paradigm. Bandura's framework posits a complex internal ability in the learner to "code" stimuli (imaginally and/or verbally), to learn complex patterns of behavior vicariously by observing socializing agents in the surrounding sub-cultural setting, their actions, and the consequences of those actions for them. Quite relevant to the negotiation network approach, some social learning research has shown that an individual chooses which among alternative socializing models to imitate based on the relative power and status of the models.

In general, Bandura's socialization (social learning) approach can be integrated with Fiske's (cultural model) externalization approach. When a given propensity for a specific cultural model is inherently ready to unfold and "show itself," socializing agents composing members of the surrounding sub-cultural setting stand ready to stimulate and reinforce that propensity. Through direct/intentional and indirect/unintentional reinforcement, an individual's earliest tendency to enact a given behavioral propensity is strengthened and shaped into a regularized action routine relevant to achieving valued benefit-outcomes in that sub-cultural setting. Therefore, within an intrinsic-communal setting, the inherent propensity to manifest "communal sharing" or "equality matching," will tend to be regularized as objective action routines (along with congruent ways of thinking and feeling). By contrast, within an extrinsic-agentic setting, the inherent propensity to display "authority ranking" or "market pricing" will tend to be regularized as overt action routines (plus appropriate modes of thinking and feeling).

In short, socializing agents representing either kind of sub-cultural setting can and will both directly (through strategies of conditioning) and indirectly and perhaps unintentionally (through serving as unwitting observational models) reinforce specific patterns of action that lead to the achievement of intrinsic/communal or extrinsic-agentic benefit-outcomes, depending upon the extant sub-cultural setting.

"Internalization" is likely to be a third significant part of the cultural shaping process. Kityama and Park (2010) provide an intriguing neuroscience approach to this aspect of cultural shaping. They argue (Kityama and Park, 2010, p. 121, Figure 1) that the macro-ecology, history, and economy of a given people shape the core values and tasks comprising the socio-cultural environment in which individuals live and act daily. Culture provides norms and expectations that stimulate the routine enactment of various behavioral tasks, and culture also provides relevant tools and problem-solving strategies. For an individual to routinely engage in such behavioral tasks, routinely using such tools and strategies, creates a distinctive pattern of neural activity, which gradually provides a distinctive structure in the brain. In other words, culturally prescribed and routine behavior feeds back to shape an individual's neurological infrastructure, which, in turn, renders a given sort of routine action pattern more probable.

Kityama and Park focus primarily on *cross-cultural* variations in the neurological internalization of culture. They suggest that the culturally prescribed routine action of a typical member of an "eastern" society creates brain patterns characteristic of an "interdependent self." In contrast, they argue, that the culturally dictated routine action of a typical member of a "western" society produces brain patterns characteristic of an "independent self." Considered in social negotiation network terms, an interdependent neurological self is motivationally predisposed to seek and achieve intrinsic-communal benefit-outcomes, while an independent neurological self is motivationally inclined to seek and obtain extrinsic-agentic benefit-outcomes. While such cross-cultural variations have been clearly identified, as we noted above, the present analysis differs from that put forth by Kityama and Park. We contend that a typical individual's culturally shaped brain is motivationally pre-disposed to seek and obtain *both* interdependence (intrinsic-communal outcomes) and independence (extrinsic-agentic outcomes), depending upon the sub-cultural setting at hand, and depending upon individual differences in cultural shaping.

Fiske's "externalization," Bandura's "socialization," and Kityama and Park's "internalization," can be linked at a general level within the social negotiation network approach. When an inherent propensity to enact a given cultural model shows itself, given appropriate external environmental stimulation by socializing agents, a culturally expected action routine will become stabilized, feeding back to shape distinctive patterns of neural pathway firing in an individual's brain. Which distinctive action routine becomes stabilized, depends upon sub-cultural setting. One kind of setting is modeled like Illustration 9: here, neurological infrastructure and action routines are shaped to motivationally predispose an individual toward actions aimed at achieving intrinsic-communal benefit-outcomes. An alternative kind of sub-cultural setting is modeled like Illustrations 7 and 8: in this instance, neurological infrastructure and action routines are shaped to motivationally predispose an individual toward action aimed at obtaining extrinsic-agentic benefit-outcomes.

6 Navigating the Practical Terrain of the Negotiation Network: Basic Mechanism

Once culturally shaped, an islander must effectively engage the varying social negotiation network micro-situations encountered across the wider island culture. We consider here what we propose as the basic mechanism through which such navigation occurs. At the heart of this mechanism is a sequential two-phase process. The first phase entails motivated cultural choice behavior, and the second phase entails post-hoc motivated reasoning (cultural cognition) about such choice behavior.

6.1 *Phase 1: Motivated Cultural Choice Behavior*

Assume an individual enters a given socio-cultural setting. The social negotiation network situation might be one that signals an opportunity to acquire either intrinsic-communal or extrinsic-agentic benefit outcomes. As the situation unfolds, the individual will make significant, situation-relevant behavioral choices across time. We argue that the longitudinal pattern of such choice behavior will be motivated. That is, in a given instance, an individual will tend to choose X over Y action based on a tacit, implicit, unconscious (gut-level sense) that choosing X will lead to a significantly valued benefit- outcome, and that choosing Y will not lead to (or actively impede the achievement of) such an outcome. For example, in a decidedly extrinsic-agentic sub-cultural situation, (see Illustration 7) islander T2 might be motivated to energetically serve the self by choosing to give T1 a relatively plain Kula article (worth relatively low prestige) saving a relatively more beautiful, more prestigious Kula artifact for a later trade, where it might yield a more valuable extrinsic-agentic benefit-outcome for the self. Or, alternatively, in a decidedly intrinsic-communal sub-cultural situation, islander T2 might choose to sacrifice the self in the service of an individual or collective other, perhaps by expending great energy making a valuable contribution to a collective division of labor aimed at preparing for a Kula expedition across the sea.

In either situation, the action choice made by T2, will be a motivated choice, a value-based choice. As such, the choice will tend to have several characteristics. First, it will tend to be a relatively "hot" (rather than "cool") choice in Zajonc's (1980) terms, meaning that it will entail relatively more emotional energy than cognitive information. Second, and similarly, this motivated choice will tend to be a relatively impulsive, automatic "go" (rather than deliberated, reasoned, "know" choice), as described by Metcalf and Mischel (1999). Third, and, again similarly, such a value-based, motivated choice will tend to be an "X-response" (reflexive response) rather than a "C-response" (reflective response) as described in Lieberman, Jarcho, and Sapute's (2004) neurological dual-processing framework.

6.2 *Phase 2: Motivated Cultural Cognition*

After an individual, say, T2 in this example has made a motivated choice, certain conditions may stimulate that individual to justify the choice behavior, to offer an account, a verbal rationale. T1 might request/demand such an account, or other members of the sub-cultural setting may call for such an account. Or, indeed, even without prompting by other parties, T2 might be moved to create a justifying account to explain the choice to the self. We suggest that the cognitive account T2 constructs will also be motivated. The explanation/justification assembled will be biased so as to promote T2's culturally shaped values. (Also see Haidt, 2001 for a somewhat similar argument). There will be a tendency to select information and assemble it quite creatively so as to arrive at a conscious cognitive destination pre-selected by an underlying automatic/unconscious value predisposition. Our view of motivated cultural cognition is similar to the analyses contributed by Kunda, 1990, Kunda, Z. and L. Sinclair, 1999;Dunning, 1999, and Snyder, 1999. However, we differ on two points. First, the cultural toolkit available to the trader is crucial. For example, the islanders in Malinowski's ethnography might well draw elements of magic, myth, and legend into the verbal-cognitive account offered to justify choice behavior. In general, non-verbal and verbal elements of explicit, socially shared knowledge (culture) will be the raw material from which an individual will draw in fashioning the justification. Second, we argue that motivated cultural cognition may be framed in either intrinsic-communal or extrinsic-agentic terms, depending upon how the negotiation network situation is framed.[16] And the same actor may well develop one kind of justification in one situation and the opposite kind of justification in a different situation, even though the two rationales are completely contradictory. As Dimaggio (1997) has persuasively argued, cultural justifications need not be, and, indeed, usually are not, logically consistent!

7 Conclusions

The foregoing analysis aimed to clarify how the automatic vs. controlled, hot vs. cold, and intrinsic-communal vs. extrinsic-agentic facets of cultural cognition operate together within a negotiation network framework informed by social neuroscience. Core features of socio-cultural settings, dynamics of shaping, and micro-situational navigation were conceptualized. Malinowski's classic Kula exchange ethnography was reviewed and "re-imagined" as a social negotiation network. Social symbolic Kula exchange, motivated by the pursuit of social prestige, was recast in terms of power-dependence dynamics in social exchange relations, networks, and groups. It was argued that an institutional cultural arrangement forms and re-forms through social negotiation. Such an arrangement was viewed as a bounded and unified "collective actor" arising from sub-institutional social exchange. It was argued that an overall societal culture is composed of distinct, varying sub-cultural settings. One important kind of setting is organized around the pursuit of intrinsic-communal benefit-outcomes, and a second important kind of setting is organized around the pursuit of extrinsic-agentic benefit-outcomes. We contended that an individual is culturally shaped through externalization, socialization, and internalization to be motivationally predisposed to seek both intrinsic-communal and extrinsic-agentic outcomes in varying sub-cultural settings. The basic mechanism underlying the navigation of a sub-cultural negotiation network setting was discussed. Phase one, it was argued, involves enacting a relatively hot, automatic value-based choice. Phase two, it was contended, entails the use of cultural content to consciously and deliberately construct a rationale to justify the choice, the trajectory of which is governed by an underlying relatively

16 Kunda (1990), Dunning (1999), and Snyder (1999) suggest that all motivated cognition as strictly self-serving. Certainly, such cognition, when it occurs in relation to an extrinsic-agentic sub-cultural setting in the service of attaining benefit- outcomes for the self, will be self-serving. However, when such cognition occurs in relation to an intrinsic- communal sub-cultural setting in the service of attaining benefit-outcomes for an individual or collective other, it will tend to be self-sacrificing and other-serving.

hot, automatic, value-position. The value-position might rest on the pursuit of either intrinsic- communal or extrinsic-agentic benefit-outcomes.

7.1 *Directions for Future Research*

Based on the analysis presented above, one direction for future research is situational framing. When and under what conditions will a motivated tendency to seek and obtain an intrinsic-communal vs. extrinsic-agentic benefit- outcome gain primacy?[17] The focus of this question is relatively short-term social negotiation network navigation, that is, navigation that occurs across varying negotiation network situations that emerge more or less continuously across relatively short spans of time. Key to this issue is the interaction of objective socio-cultural situation and individual cultural cognition. In pursuit of this research concern, the potential connection between the social negotiation network framework and some facets of "ecological psychology" should be explored. Perhaps Gibson's (1977) classic ecological notion of "affordance" comes into play. From an individual's perspective, as a given situation begins to take shape, its objective features potentially become apparent and available for use. As the situational configuration reaches a meaningful threshold, its features "afford" either an intrinsic-communal or extrinsic-agentic action routine. Simultaneously, the individual's culturally shaped predispositions affect the inclination to see (or fail to see) the opportunity afforded by the emerging situation, thus helping to bring (or failing to bring) the situation into a specific shape. One individual's motivational bent toward achieving intrinsic-communal benefit-outcomes might trigger a response to situational "affordances" one way (perhaps by seizing and using a relevant opportunity, perhaps to sacrifice self for an individual or collective other). A second individual's motivational inclination toward extrinsic-agentic benefit-outcomes might cue a response to the same situational "affordances" in a different way, perhaps missing the relevant opportunity, indeed, perhaps by enacting an extrinsic-agentic behavioral choice instead. Future research should pursue this line of thought.

A second direction for future research concerns relatively longer-term navigation across the negotiation network. A key question is: How does an individual navigate the varying sub-cultural settings of the social negotiation network with greater or lesser success? "Success," we argue, can be reckoned in terms of the relative level of benefit-outcomes an individual achieves.

---

17 Pursuing this question would extend earlier work on framing social values (Stolte and Fender, 2007).

Clearly, the constitution of objective success will vary by sub-cultural setting. Also, an individual islander's relative success in achieving benefit-outcomes will probably depend on the interaction of both the culturally shaped self the islander brings into the sub-cultural setting and the objective logic of action operating in that setting. Thus, for example, objective success in a socio-cultural setting like the stratified negotiation network shown in Illustration 7 can be reasonably figured in terms of Kula-borne social prestige. If, through social exchange, T2 possesses relatively more prestige than T1 at the end of the day, T2 can be reasonably said to be objectively more successful than T1. However, within a different socio-cultural situation such as the negotiation network situation shown in Illustration 9, objective success might be measured not in terms of Kula social prestige, but rather in terms of the level of collective-specific social approval (more like group-relevant social esteem) an islander attains in exchange for that islander's contributions to the collective division of labor. If, compared with other islanders in Illustration 9, T12 spends relatively greater effort, making a relatively more valuable contribution to the success of a productive exchange group, T12 may be allocated relatively more social esteem by colleagues. Compared with T12's colleagues, T12 can thereby be said to be relatively more successful in that socio-cultural setting.

Consider the probable fates of three island traders across two contrasting social negotiation network scenarios, again drawing images from Malinowski's Kula ethnography.

First consider island trader T1. Assume T1 has been culturally shaped to value more highly intrinsic-communal than extrinsic-agentic benefit-outcomes. T1's chronic tendency is to make motivated choices and adduce motivated justifications favoring self-sacrifice for individual or collective others. It is in fact difficult for T1 to make self-serving choices or give self-serving justifications.

Second, consider island trader T2. Assume T2 been culturally shaped to value more highly extrinsic-agentic than the intrinsic-communal benefit-outcomes. T2's chronic tendency is to exhibit motivated choices and motivated cultural cognition in the service of the self. It is hard for T2 to make other-serving choices and adduce other-serving justifications.

Third, consider island trader T3. Assume T3 has been culturally shaped to equally value intrinsic-communal and extrinsic-agentic benefit-outcomes. T3 is able flexibly to switch between the two sorts of motivated choice and motivated cultural cognition, depending on the objective requirements of the socio-cultural situation at hand. However, assume that while T3 can evince behavioral choice and cultural justification fitting either value position, each value position softens somewhat the effect of the opposite value position.

7.2 *Scenario 1: Cultural Cognition and Relative Success in a Stratified Negotiation Network*

Suppose the current socio-cultural situation takes on the character depicted in Illustration 7, the stratified and open negotiation network. Success in this context is the magnitude of social prestige an individual trader can amass relative to other traders via the Kula trading process. The objective, matter-of-fact, operative "logic of action" is "competition." To successfully obtain relatively valuable Kula articles worth relatively high levels of social prestige will depend upon vigorous self-serving agency as an adept Kula negotiator/competitor in such a situation. It is reasonable to suppose that a culturally instituted social exchange situation like that represented by Illustration 7 will lead to different levels of objective success for traders, T1, T2, and T3. We predict that Kula social prestige will be ordered among these three individuals as follows: T2 > T3 > T1.

This prediction follows from the ways in which the three culturally shaped traders connect with the objective socio-cultural social negotiation network situation at hand. Trader T2, an independent/individualistic individual, whose strong chronic internal bent is to make motivated behavioral choices and motivated justifications evincing extrinsic-agency, is likely to best fit the competitive stratified negotiation network situation. T2 is likely to gain the most beautiful Kula articles, to achieve the most social prestige. Trader T3 is predicted to come next in the order. While T3 is flexible, and while T3 can make motivated choices and give motivated reasons in the direction of both value complexes, his/her chronic orientation toward taking an extrinsic-agentic value position is likely to be softened to some degree by a simultaneous chronic orientation toward taking an intrinsic-communal value position. Thus, T3 will not be as successful in accumulating highly artistic Kula articles and social prestige as T2. However, T3 will tend to be objectively more successful than T1, who's culturally shaped psyche oriented most strongly toward an intrinsic-communal value position and weakly toward extrinsic-agency value position.

7.3 *Scenario 2: Cultural Cognition and Relative Success in a Productive Exchange System*

By contrast, suppose the current socio-cultural situation takes on the character pictured in Illustration 9, the unified productive exchange system, based on a division of labor. Success in this alternative context is the magnitude of social approval (sense of acceptance by and group-relevant esteem) allocated by colleagues committed to a shared effort (a dangerous Kula journey across rough seas). The objective, matter-of-fact operative "logic of action" here is cooperation. To successfully acquire gestures communicating a relatively high level of esteem will depend upon vigorous self-subordination/self-sacrifice in support of the collective benefit of one's fellow traders. One would reasonably expect that a culturally instituted social exchange situation like that shown in Figure 1C will lead to different levels of objective success for traders T1, T2, and T3. We predict that signs/gestures of group member approval/esteem will be ordered as follows: T1 > T3 > T2.

We make these predictions based on how the three culturally shaped island traders mesh with this alternative socio-cultural negotiation network situation. Trader T1 is culturally shaped to have a strong chronic internal bent to make motivated choices and adduce motivated reasons displaying intrinsic-communal values. Therefore, T1 is likely to best fit the cooperative productive exchange situation. T1 is likely to earn the highest level of group approval/esteem for personal self-sacrifice on behalf of the group's collective goal. Again, trader T3 is likely to end up next in the order, for essentially the same reason as stated above. While T3 is flexible and while T3 can make motivated choices and give motivated reasons in the direction of both intrinsic-communal and extrinsic-agentic values, the latter value position offsets the former value position somewhat. Thus, T3 will not be as successful in earning group approval/esteem for his contributions to the collective task. However, T3 will be more objectively successful in garnering group approval/esteem in this setting than trader T2, whose culturally shaped and chronic bent is most strongly toward extrinsic-agentic benefit-outcomes and only weakly toward intrinsic- communal benefit-outcomes. The predictions following from this line of reasoning ought to be probed and tested in follow-up empirical research.

8 Summary

The core questions and issues that have been examined in this chapter can be briefly encapsulated as follows: How do automatic vs. controlled, hot vs. cold, and agentic vs. communal facets of cultural cognition operate together in a perspective informed by social neuroscience? This question was explored by re-imagining Malinowski's classic ethnographic case study of the Kula in light of the general process theory serving as the backdrop of this monograph. We proposed: (1) sub-institutional patterns of structural power-dependence form a foundation for the rise of tacit/implicit meanings, which evolve through social negotiation into explicit/shared, cultural meaning agreements; (2) crucial sub- cultural categories form around the pursuit of both agentic benefits and communal benefits; (3) an individual is culturally shaped through externalization, socialization, and internalization to value and be motivated to seek both kinds of benefits; (4) an individual faces the existential task of navigating both agentic and communal situations across the negotiation network; (5) the basic individual mechanism underlying such navigation entails motivated behavioral choice and motivated cultural cognition; (6) a behavioral choice rests on automatic, largely implicit and hot cognitive processing; (7) motivated cultural cognition rests mostly on the deliberate, mostly explicit, and cool selection of materials from the prevailing cultural toolkit for assembling a justification, but whose underlying trajectory is biased by an automatic, hot value-position, whether agentic or communal. Based on the analysis, we also proposed some potentially useful directions for future empirical research.

References

Abele, A. E. and Wojciszke, B. (2007) Agency and communion from the perspective of self versus others. *Journal of Personality and Social Psychology* 93, 5:751–763.

Bakan, D. (1966) The Duality of Human Existence. Reading, PA: Addison Wesley.

Baldwin, J. and Baldwin, J. (1978) Behaviorism and Erkldren. *American Sociological Review* 43, 3:335–347.

Bandura, A. (1986) Social Foundations of Thought and Action: A Social Cognitive Theory. Englewood Cliffs: Prentice-Hall.

Barth, F. (1966) Models of Social Organization. London: Royal Anthropological Institute.

Batson, C.D. (1987) Prosocial motivation: Is it ever truly altruistic? *Advances in Experimental Social Psychology* 20:65–122.

Cerulo, K.A. (2002) Culture in Mind: Toward A Sociology of Culture and Cognition. New York: Routledge.

Cerulo, K.A. (2014) Continuing the story: Maximizing the intersections of cognitive science and sociology. *Sociological Forum* 29, 4:1012–1019.

Clark, M.S. and Mills, J. (1993) The difference between communal and exchange relationships: What it is and is not. *Personality and Social Psychology Bulletin* 19, 6:684–691.

Clark, M.S. and Mills, J. (1979) Interpersonal attraction in exchange and communal relationships. *Journal of Personality and Social Psychology* 37, 1:12–24.

Clark, M. and Finkel, E.J. (2005) Willingness to express emotion: The Impact of relationship type, communal orientation, and their interaction. *Personal Relationships* 12, 2:169–180.

Dimaggio, P. (1997) Culture and cognition. *Annual Review of Sociology* 23, 1:263–287.

Dimaggio, P. (2002) Why cognitive (and cultural) sociology needs cognitive psychology. In K.A. Cerulo (ed.) Culture in Mind: Toward a Sociology of Culture and Cognition, 274–284. New York: Routledge.

Dunning, D. (1999) A newer look: Motivated social cognition and the schematic representation of social concepts. *Psychological Inquiry* 10, 1:1–11.

Emerson, R.M. (1972) Exchange Theory, part II: Exchange relations and networks. In J. Berger, M. Zelditch, and B. Anderson (eds.) Sociological Theories in Progress, Vol. 2, 3–87, Boston: Houghton-Mifflin.

Emerson, R.M. (1969) Operant psychology and exchange theory. In R.L. Burgess and D. Bushell (eds.) The Experimental Analysis of Social Processes: Implications for a Behavioral Sociology, 42–69, New York: Columbia University Press.

Emerson, R.M. (1962) Power-dependence relations. *American Sociological Review* 27, 3:31–40.

Emerson, R.M. (1976) Social exchange theory. *Annual Review of Sociology* 51, 3:335–362.

Emerson, R.M. (1981) Social exchange theory. In M. Turner and R. Rosenberg (eds.) Social Psychology: Sociological Perspectives, 81–113. New York: Basic Books.

Evans, J.B. (2008) Dual-processing accounts of reasoning, judgment, and social cognition. *Annual Review of Psychology* 59, 4:255–78.

Fiske, A.P. (1991) Structures of Social Life: The Four Elementary Forms of Life. New York: Free Press.

Fiske, A.P., Kityama, M., Markus, H., and Nisbett, R. (1998) The cultural matrix of social psychology. In S. Fiske, G. Lindzey, and D. Gilbert (eds.) Handbook of Social Psychology, 915–981. Boston: McGraw-Hill.

Gibson, J.J. (1977) The Theory of Affordances. In Perceiving, Knowing, and Acting: Toward an Ecological Psychology. In R. Bransford and J. Shaw (eds.), 127–143. Hillsdale: Lawrence Erlbaum.

Gul, F. and Pesendorfer, W. (2005) The Case for Mindless Economics. Princeton: Princeton University.

Haidt, J. (2001) The emotional dog and its rational tail: a social intuitionist approach to moral judgment. *Psychological Review*, 814–834.

Kityama, S. and Park, J. (2010) Cultural neuroscience of the self: Understanding the social grounding of the brain. *Social Cognitive Affective Neuroscience*, 111–129.

Kohlberg, L. (1969) Stage and sequence: The cognitive-developmental approach. In D. Goslin (ed.) Handbook of Socialization Theory and Research. Chicago: Rand McNally.

Kunda, Z. (1990). The case for motivated reasoning. *Psychological Bulletin*, 108, 3, 480–498.

Kunda, Z. and Sinclair, L. (1999) Motivated reasoning with stereotypes: Activation, application, and inhibition. *Psychological Inquiry*, 12–22.

Lieberman, M., Jarcho, J., and Satpute, A. (2004) Evidence-based and intuition-based self-knowledge: An fMRI Study. *Journal of Personality and Social Psychology*, 421–435.

Lowenstein, G., Scott, R., and Cohen, J. (2008) Neuroeconomics. *Annual Review of Psychology*, 647–72.

Malinowski, B. (1920) Kula: The circulating exchange of valuables in the archipelagoes of Eastern New Guinea. *Man*, 97–105.

Markus, H. and Kityama, S. (1991) Culture and self: Implications for cognition, emotion, and motivation. *Psychological Review*, 224–253.

Mead, G.H. (1934). Mind, Self, and Society. Chicago: University of Chicago Press.

Metcalfe, J. and Mischel, W. (1999) A hot/cool-system analysis of delay of gratification: Dynamics of willpower. *Psychological Review* 106:3–19.

Paivio, A. (2007) Mind and Its Evolution: A Dual Coding Theoretical Approach. Mahwah: Erlbaum.

Piaget, J. (1958) The Moral Judgment of the Child. New York: Free Press.

Sahlins, M. (2000) Culture in Practice. New York: Zone Books New York.

Sanday, P.R. (1979) The ethnographic paradigms. *Administrative Science Quarterly*, 527–538.

Snyder, R. (1999) Reality negotiations: Motivated strategies underlying judgments of oneself and other people. *Psychological Inquiry*, 69–72.

Stolte, J.F. and Fender, S. (2007) Framing Social Values: An Experimental Study of Culture and Cognition. *Social Psychology Quarterly*, 59–69.

Stolte, J.F. and Emerson, R.M. (1977) Structural inequality: Position and power in network structures. In R.L. Hamblin and J. Kunkel (eds.) Behavioral Theory in Sociology: Essays in Honor of George C. Homans, 117–139. New Brunswick, NJ: Transaction.

Stolte, J.F. (2000) Beyond the concept of value in power-dependence theory: expanding a model of the whole actor. *Advances in Group Processes*, 179–202.

Stolte, J.F. (1988) From micro- to macro-exchange structure: Measuring power imbalance at the exchange network level. *Social Psychology Quarterly*, 357–364.

Stolte, J.F. (1990) Power processes in structures of dependence and exchange. *Advances in Group Processes* 7:129–150.

Stolte, J.F. (1992) Review of structures of social life: The four elementary forms of social life by A.P. Fiske. *American Journal of Sociology*, 1194–1196.

Stolte, J.F. (1987) The formation of justice norms. *American Sociological Review*, 774–784.

Stolte, J.F. (1983) The legitimation of structural inequality: Reformulation and test of the self- evaluation argument. *American Sociological Review*, 331–342.

Vygotsky, L. (1962) Thought and Language. Cambridge: MIT Press.

Wolf, K.H. (1950) The Sociology of George Simmel. Glencoe: The Free Press.

Wrong, D. (1961) The Over-socialized conception of man in modern sociology. *American Sociological Review*, 183–193.

Zajonc, R.B. (1980) Feeling and thinking: Preferences need no inferences. *American Psychologist*, 151–175.

CHAPTER 4

Measurement and Social Desirability Response Bias in Experimental Vignette Research

Vignette research methods have been widely used to study a diverse set of research issues, including: clinical decision-making (Evans, Roberts, Keeley, Blossom, Amaro, Garcia, Stough, Canter, Robles, and Reed, 2014), medical ethics (Fitzgerald and Hurst, 2017), nurse decision-making (Kada, 2017) factorial survey design (Teti, Gross, Knoll, and Bluher, 2016), policy politics (Remler and Van Ryzin, 2015) public health (Guest and Namey, 2014) philosophy and law (Zamir and Teichman, 2014) topics in social psychology (Stolte, 1994; Stolte and Fender, 2007) perceptions of Alzheimer's disease (Berry, Williams, Thomas, and Blair, 2015) and judgments of filial responsibility (Santoro, Van Liew, Holloway, McKinnon, Little, and Cronan, 2016), among many other empirical issues.

As Evans et al. (2014) note, two major quantitative uses of vignette methodology are the factorial survey and the traditional experimental design. The factorial survey incorporates randomized vignettes in large-scale descriptive social surveys, simultaneously seeking to achieve both internal and external validity of results (Rossi and Nock, 1982). In traditional experimental designs, vignettes are used to test causal hypotheses derived from abstract, scope-defined, general process theories, and internal validity is given primacy. Although these two approaches have different goals and use different tactics, they both provide useful and complementary empirical knowledge.

In both approaches, vignettes are designed to create hypothetical cultural/normative contexts in which self-reported attitudes (thoughts, feelings, judgments, behavioral intentions) are measured. A key potential problem often arising in such self-report research is social desirability response bias. In essence, such bias arises when respondents or subjects deliberately construct and display an attitude motivated to obtain the social approval of an external audience rather than automatically displaying a less controlled attitude motivated by a personal tendency/preference/value. Often such bias distorts the meaning of empirical results and leads to erroneous conclusions.[1]

1 It has often been argued that a personally held attitude displayed automatically is more "real" and "authentic" than an attitude displayed deliberately to obtain the approval of an external audience, the latter being merely a "performance." But Fazio's theory (Fazio and Olson,

 | DOI:10.1163/9789004713918_005

Social desirability response bias is especially likely to arise when self-reported attitudes are measured within a "socially sensitive," "problematic" cultural/normative context. Such contexts entail ethical dilemmas, ideological/political differences, racial, gender, class, and sexual identity differences, and various kinds of stigma (e.g., mental disability, drug use, sexual preferences/behavior). Today, for instance, many scholars are focused on issues of inequality and equity in various realms, including health. Such issues are more than likely to be "sensitive" or "problematic" for respondents.

As Evans et al. (2014:164–165) note, vignette methods can play a useful role in dealing with social desirability response bias. Such methods provide a flexible tool for "asking questions and inferring conclusions indirectly." The present study builds upon and expands this insight, pursuing a particular pathway for clarifying and dealing with social desirability response bias in vignette research. The central purpose of the present study is to report a vignette experimental test of a dual-process theory linking self-reported attitude measurement, socially sensitive contexts, and social desirability response bias. The research uses a sample of university students. The primary objective in the study presented here is a strong, experimental test of a theory, maximizing confidence in causal inference and the internal validity of results. Building on this platform, later research can and should extend focus to external validity and a wider generalizability of results, perhaps using the factorial survey approach.

In the discussion below: (a) Fazio's dual process theory is summarized, (b) an hypothesis derived from the theory is specified, (c) the method, subjects, and procedure of a vignette experimental test of the hypothesis are described, (d) the results are presented, and (e) the findings are summarized, noting their limitations, and making suggestions for further research.

1 Framework: MODE Theory

Fazio and his colleagues (Fazio, 1990; Fazio and Olson, 2003) formulated the MODE ("motivation and opportunity as determinants") framework within

2003), elaborated below, argues that both attitude displays are "real" and "authentic." They are motivated by different goals. The essential problem is erroneously construing an attitude motivated by social desirability as an attitude motivated instead by a personally held attitude. To avoid distortion and confusion in research results, the two kinds of attitude display must be clearly distinguished and monitored, and inferences from the data must be carefully and accurately made.

a broader body of dual-process theories in social psychology (Chaiken and Trope, 1999).

Consider a hypothetical vignette experiment focused on a clinician's medical decision- making. Suppose she/he must decide to recommend for or against a very expensive treatment. Imagine that the vignettes developed for this experiment are identical in describing a hypothetical patient's characteristics except for the patient's age, which is experimentally manipulated: condition A describes the patient as 35 years of age, while condition B describes the patient as 87 years of age. Based on all other patient characteristics except age, suppose best medical practice clearly dictates that treatment should be recommended. Will the clinician's decision be based only on the prescribed best practice? Or will it be influenced by a diffuse, often distorted but widely held and prejudicial age stereotype?

Age, along with many other personal traits (race, gender, socioeconomic status, ethnicity, sexual identity, etc.) may make a hypothetical vignette context "socially sensitive" and "problematic." Depending upon her/his past experience, a clinician may have acquired strong and rigid stereotypes linked to various personal traits and/or social situations. For example, in this hypothetical study, the clinician may react strongly to an age-based stereotype, judging the 87-year-old patient as "too old" compared to the 35-year-old patient for recommending the expensive medical treatment.

Within Fazio's MODE framework, a key distinction is made between (a) cognitive processing that is spontaneous and automatic and (b) cognitive processing that is deliberate and controlled. Within vignette condition A (where the patient's age is 87) the clinician might be influenced by the age stereotype and decide spontaneously and automatically against recommending treatment.

On the other hand, the clinician might not base her/his decision spontaneously on an age stereotype. Instead, she/he might engage in more deliberate/controlled cognitive processing. In this process, her/his attention might come increasingly to focus on the "socially sensitive," problematic, nature of the broader context surrounding the medical decision. Some part of the vignette-mediated situation might move the clinician to deeply consider the many complex issues surrounding the decision to be taken into account. Perhaps, among these issues are how the wider medical profession, government guidelines, and people in general view and react to old age prejudice in the context of health care decisions. After weighing such considerations, the clinician might decide to override his/her initial impulse and respond in a manner calculated to obtain the social approval of these various external audiences. In the end, her/his deliberate and controlled cognitive processing might result in a medical decision in which the patient's age is treated as completely irrelevant. She/he might decide that only the medically mandated best practice must be followed. On this basis, he/she might (reluctantly but resolvedly) decide to recommend treatment.

MODE theory argues that the two cognitive processes, spontaneous-automatic and deliberate-controlled, are often "mixed" across time. Upon initial reading of the vignette in condition A (the "age 87" condition), the clinician might be influenced by the age stereotype and start to form a decision against recommending treatment. However, before formally recording his/her decision, she/he might begin to grapple with an increasingly uncomfortable quandary, leading to a revision of the initial decision. All things considered, she/he might decide age must be treated as irrelevant: she/he might, in the end, recommend treatment in accord with best practice. In MODE theory, spontaneous-automatic and deliberate-controlled cognitive processes often work back and forth together dynamically across time to result in a given decision. Such dual processing is especially likely when a context presents a significant dilemma or is otherwise socially problematic.

MODE theory argues that the outcome of cognitive processing underlying a decision will depend upon the interplay of two basic factors: motivation and opportunity. In this hypothetical illustration, one significant source of motivation is a personally held attitude motivated by age-prejudice. That is, due to past social learning and life experience, the clinician may be strongly motivated by an internalized age stereotype. If the experimental vignette provides an opportunity favoring the display of such prejudice, the theory predicts she/he will decide quickly and automatically to recommend against treatment for the 87-year-old patient, despite prescribed best medical practice.

However, a second significant source of motivation is the desire to obtain the social approval of the medical community, contingent upon following best practice guidelines. If the experimental vignette provides an opportunity favoring the display of a self-impression that will achieve such approval, the theory predicts that she/he will override the initial spontaneous impulse and decide to recommend treatment, in line with best medical practice norms.

In short, a personal attitude of age prejudice is only *one* source of motivation. The expected reaction of the wider medical community is *an alternative* source of motivation. A clinician strongly motivated by age prejudice, initially leaning toward recommending against treatment, but who, upon controlled and deliberate cognitive processing, decides to recommend treatment in accord with best practice can be said to have decided on the basis of *social desirability.*[2] Vignette-mediated motivation and opportunity combine to shape the final decision.

Importantly, in Fazio's framework *the way a self-reported attitude is measured* is crucial for determining the opportunity facet of the situation shaping cognitive processing and decision-making. If an *explicit measuring instrument* is used, deliberate-controlled processing tends to be encouraged and facilitated. Administering such an instrument arouses and directs a subject's attention to the research and researcher as well as the broader socially sensitive context, activates deliberate cognitive processing, and creates an opportunity to construct a performance motivated by a desire to obtain external social approval. Such motivation pushes a subject to invest more cognitive resources in considering the sensitive issues surrounding the decision.

In the hypothetical illustration, measuring the clinician's attitude explicitly increases the likelihood of a socially desirable decision: even though personally reluctant, she/he is more likely to follow best practice and recommend medical treatment. By contrast, MODE theory argues that the use of an *implicit measuring instrument* encourages and facilitates spontaneous-automatic cognitive processing. A different decision is likely to be reached. Implicit measurement diminishes the attention a subject is likely to give to what is going on in the research and the broader, "sensitive" and "problematic" facets of the situation. Such measurement instead creates an opportunity favoring quick, automatic, spontaneous cognitive processing. Under implicit measurement, the clinician, assuming she/he is motivated by significant age-prejudice, is likely to recommend against treatment for the older patient.

In sum, MODE theory suggests: in hypothetical "socially sensitive" and "problematic" decision contexts created by vignette methods: (a) measuring self-reported attitudes explicitly leads to more social desirability responding, while (b) measuring self-reported attitudes implicitly leads to less social desirability responding.

The vignette experiment to which we now turn was designed to test this theory.

---

2 If a researcher's goal is to study age prejudice in healthcare decision-making, but if subjects/respondents hide their strong personally held age-prejudicial attitudes, revealing only a socially desirable non-prejudicial response in order to obtain medical community approval, and if the researcher misconstrues these results as showing an actually low level of age prejudice, then such social desirability response bias leads to a seriously inaccurate empirical conclusion.

2 Method

2.1 *Subjects*

In exchange for extra course credit, students (N = 149) volunteered to serve as participants in what was described as a "study of social perceptions." Subjects included undergraduate (N = 137) and graduate (N = 12) students. Subjects included females (N = 133) and males (N = 16). All 149 subjects responded to a post-experimental questionnaire instrument, and the whole dataset was used for part of the analysis reported below. However, only a subset of the whole group of subjects (N = 55), after responding to the post-experimental questionnaire, also wrote open-ended essays about the central vignette character (N of Females = 49; N of Males = 6). Part of the analysis described below was based on the whole dataset, and another part of the analysis was based on the smaller data-subset.[3]

2.2 *Procedure*

The present study created a "socially sensitive" and "problematic" cultural/normative context by using modified versions of vignettes developed in an earlier study (Stolte and Fender, 2007). In general, the context involves a family dilemma/quandary regarding how best to provide care for an aging family member suffering from early-onset Alzheimer's disease.

Across the vignettes, a central character is portrayed as an adult child of an aging parent. In one set of vignettes, the central character and the impaired elderly parent are depicted as female. In another set of vignettes, the central character and the disabled elderly parent are portrayed as male. In one set of vignettes, the motive underlying a caregiving decision made by the central character is depicted as selfless family affection. In another set of vignettes, the motive behind the caregiving decision is painted as the self-interested pursuit of money.

The vignettes were designed in part to create a hypothetical clash of cultural norms and expectations concerning the appropriateness of making a "communal" (selfless-family-affection-based) vs. an "agentic" (material self-interest-based) decision in reference to providing caregiving to an afflicted elderly family member (Able and Wojciszke, 2007). In addition, the vignettes were designed to examine the effects of gender, a "socially sensitive" and "problematic" characteristic, across the vignette-mediated cultural/normative context.

3 Because laboratory space with e-mail capacity and other logistical resources were limited, it was feasible to collect written essay data from only this smaller subset (N = 55) of subjects.

Within such a context, how will subjects react to a caregiving decision made by a female vs. male central character? Much past research has shown pervasive impact of a broad gender stereotype: women are depicted as and expected to be "communal," while men are portrayed as and expected to be "agentic." Generally in the past, actors and social situations falling into line with this gender stereotype have tended to be socially approved. Historically, actors and social situations deviating from this stereotype have tended to be socially disapproved (Davis, S. & Greenstein, T., 2009, Eagly, A., 1987). How will the gender stereotype link to other facets of the vignette-mediated cultural/normative situation to influence the level of approval bestowed on the central character?

We turn to a detailed description of the study protocol:

After reading, dating, and signing an informed consent document approved by a university IRB-Committee, a subject was randomly assigned to one of the following four experimental vignette conditions:

2.2.1 Vignette Condition 1: Female/Communal (FC)

Consider the following two people:

Young Female photo	Middle aged Female photo

These photos are of a daughter (first photo) and her mother (second photo).

Recently, the older woman's (the mother's) health and mind have begun to decline, because she has been diagnosed with early-onset Alzheimer's disease. Physicians have indicated that they expect the mother's dementia to worsen over time to the point where she will not recognize her daughter.

At the present time, the mother needs a lot of help and support with the basic activities of daily living … eating, bathing, dressing, walking, round-the-clock supervision, etc. In light of her mother's plight, the daughter is considering what decisions to make.

After struggling with all the issues, the daughter finally decides to have her mother move into her own home, so that she (the daughter) can care directly for all her mother's needs. The daughter is moved to make this decision mainly in light of her high personal regard for and strong devotion to her mother. The daughter knows this decision will make her own life substantially more burdensome than placing her mother in a skilled nursing facility, but the daughter places her mother's welfare above her own, and simply wants to express her great affection for her mother.

2.2.2 Vignette Condition 2: Female/Agentic (FA)

Consider the following two people:

Young Female photo	Middle Aged Female photo

These photos are of a daughter (first photo) and her mother (second photo).

Recently, the older woman's (the mother's) health and mind have begun to decline, because she has been diagnosed with early-onset Alzheimer's disease. Physicians have indicated that they expect the mother's dementia to worsen over time to the point where she will not recognize her daughter.

At the present time, the mother needs a lot of help and support with the basic activities of daily living ... eating, bathing, dressing, walking, round-the-clock supervision, etc. In light of her mother's plight, the daughter is considering what decisions to make.

After struggling with all the issues, the daughter finally decides to have her mother move into her own home, so that she (the daughter) can care directly for all her mother's needs. The daughter is moved to make this decision mainly in light of practical economic circumstances. The daughter knows that this decision will cost much less than placing her mother in a skilled nursing facility, and the daughter strongly wants to conserve her mother's wealth, so that when the mother dies, her (the daughter's) inheritance will be much greater than it would be otherwise.

2.2.3 Vignette Condition 3: Male/Communal (MC)

Consider the following two people:

Young Male photo	Middle aged Male photo

These photos are of a son (first photo) and his father (second photo).

Recently, the older man's (the father's) health and mind have begun to decline, because he has been diagnosed with early-onset Alzheimer's disease. Physicians have indicated that they expect the father's dementia to worsen over time to the point where he will not recognize his son.

At the present time, the father needs a lot of help and support with the basic activities of daily living ... eating, bathing, dressing, walking, round-the-clock supervision, etc. In light of his father's plight, the son is considering what decisions to make.

After struggling with all the issues, the son finally decides to have his father move into his own home, so that he (the son) can care directly for all his father's needs. The son is moved to make this decision mainly in light of his high personal regard for and strong devotion to his father. The son knows this decision will make his own life substantially more burdensome than placing his father in a skilled nursing facility, but the son places his father's welfare above his own, and simply wants to express his great affection for his father.

2.2.4 Vignette Condition 4: Male/Agentic (MA)

Consider the following two people:

Young Male photo	Middle Aged Male photo

These photos are of a son (first photo) and his father (second photo).

Recently, the older man's (the father's) health and mind have begun to decline, because he has been diagnosed with early-onset Alzheimer's disease. Physicians have indicated that they expect the father's dementia to worsen over time to the point where he will not recognize his son. At the present time, the father needs a lot of help and support with the basic activities of daily living ... eating, bathing, dressing, walking, round-the-clock supervision, etc. In light of his father's plight, the son is considering what decisions to make.

After struggling with all the issues, the son finally decides to have his father move into his own home, so that he (the son) can care directly for all his father's needs. The son is moved to make this decision mainly in light of practical economic circumstances. The son knows that this decision will cost much less than placing his father in a skilled nursing facility, and the son strongly wants to conserve his father's wealth, so that when the father dies, his (the son's) inheritance will be much greater than it would be otherwise.

To examine the effects of these experimentally manipulated vignette conditions on subjects' reactions to the central character, we used the level of social approval subjects expressed in reference to the central vignette character as the dependent variable. As a broad concept, such social approval captures much of the general idea beneath the term, "social desirability." As an abstract concept, social approval might be indicated by using different measuring instruments. Varying measures might be equally plausible conceptually, and each might meet a reasonable standard of face validity.

The present experiment used two contrasting instruments for measuring subjects' approval of the central vignette character. The first is an explicit measure. The second is an implicit measure.

To measure social approval *explicitly*, we employed a widely used scale developed by Aron, Aron, Tudor, and Nelson (1991). This scale measures the "incorporation of other into self" (denoted as "IOS" in the discussion below). The younger family member (adult son or adult daughter) was designated as the central vignette character to be evaluated by subjects.

For IOS, the experimental instructions were as follows:

"Consider the person shown in the first photo above (the photo of the younger person). Now please examine the diagrams below. Imagine you are "self" and the younger person in the photo above is "other." Please circle the diagram which best describes how you feel about your relationship to that "other" person." This scale is made up of seven pairs of Venn Diagrams, showing variable overlap and depicting varying levels of emotional identification with (social approval of) the other, from low to high. After a subject responded by circling a given pair of diagrams, the response was translated into a number from 1 = low to 7 = high emotional identification with (approval of) the central vignette character.

By contrast, to measure social approval *implicitly*, the Linguistic Inquiry and Word Count (LIWC) program (Tausczik and Pennebaker, 2010) was used to measure the proportion of positive emotion-words used by subjects in open-ended essays written to imaginatively describe various facets of the central character's life (denoted as POSEMO In the discussion below).

For POSEMO, experimental instructions were as follows: "In reference to the person shown in the first photo above (the younger person), please write a 250–350-word essay describing what you imagine that person's family, work, friendship, religion, politics, civic activity, and recreation are like."[4]

4 In developing MODE theory, Fazio and his associates (Fazio, 1990) focused on several implicit measuring instruments, especially the "implicit association test" (IAT), developed by Greenwald and Banaji (1995). The IAT and similar measures, rest on response latency as a way of implicitly capturing attitude-to-behavior constructs. The present experiment relies instead on the Linguistic Inquiry and Word Count (LIWC) approach developed by Pennebaker and his colleagues (Pennebaker, J.W. Chung, C.K., Ireland, M., Gonzales, A., and Booth, R.J., 2007; Tausczik, Y and J. Pennebaker, 2010) and used widely by many others. LIWC, in contrast to IAT, measures a concept implicitly by indicating facets of cognitive processing upon which a subject is not directly focusing his/her *attention*. When referring to the central character in the vignettes, we take POSEMO to be a spontaneous-automatic rather than deliberate-controlled display of attitude.

2.3 *Hypothesis*

The procedure described above, including the explicit and implicit measures, was used to test of this prediction:

Measuring the social approval displayed toward a central vignette character explicitly (as IOS) will result in more social desirability responding than measuring such approval implicitly (as POSEMO).

3 Results

3.1 *Effect of Vignette Manipulation on the Explicit Measure: IOS*

As expected, the vignette manipulation had a significant effect on IOS [F (3, 145) = 13.838, p = .000]. Mean IOS is significantly greater in reference to the "communal" (selfless-family-affection-motivated) than "agentic" (material-self-interested money-motivated) central vignette character, as can be seen in Illustration 10.[5]

Crucially, Illustration 10 shows no significant differences in IOS by gender variations across vignettes. A post-hoc multiple comparison analysis showed no significant difference between FC and MC and no significant difference between FA and MA. Instead, only the central vignette character's decision-making motive, "agentic" (self-interested money-motivated) vs. "communal," (selfless-family-affection-motivated), regardless of gender, determined variation in IOS. This finding is discussed more fully below.

3.2 *Effect of Vignette Manipulation on the Implicit Measure: POSEMO*

The data show the vignette manipulation had a significant effect on POSEMO [F (3, 51) = 3.11, p = .000]. However, it is the specific pattern of this effect shown in Illustration 11 as compared with the results for IOS shown in Illustration 10 that provides strong support for the hypothesis. In this instance, gender variations across vignettes did have a large impact. The largest difference shown in Illustration 11 is that between the female communal (FC) central character and male agentic (MA) central character. In a post-hoc multiple comparison analysis, this difference is significant [*Tukey HSD* = .026]. As the data in Illustration 11 show, the female communal (FC) character is allocated the highest and the male agentic (MA) character the lowest levels of POSEMO. Yet, a

5 The present study was unable to determine whether or not subject gender had an effect. Specifically, the student population from which the experimental subject pool was selected is sharply skewed demographically, with females (experimental N = 133) substantially outnumbering males (experimental N = 16).

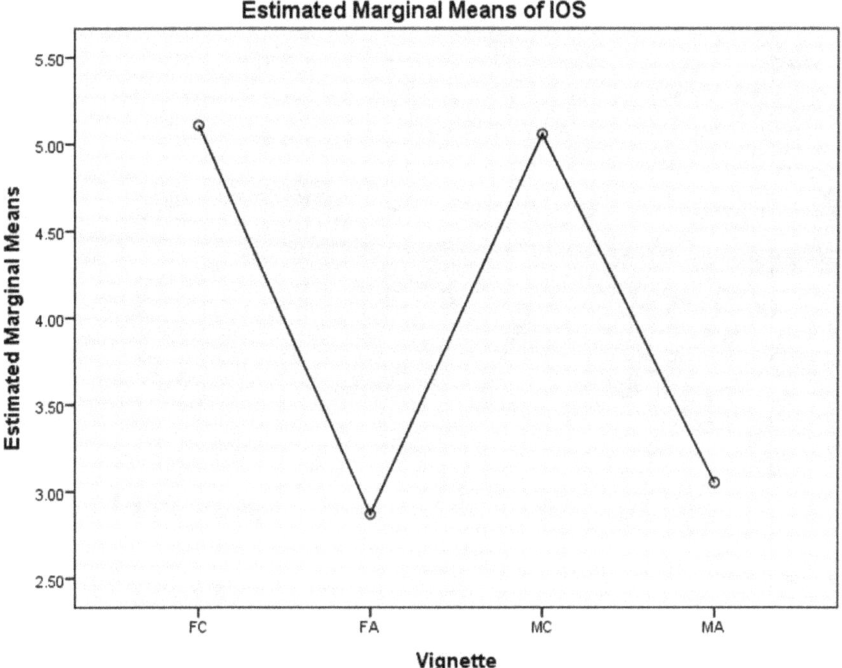

FC = female-communal (*SD*

2.02*) FA = female-agentic (*SD

***1.79*) MC = male-communal**

(*SD 2.10*) MA = male-agentic

(*SD 2.13*)

ILLUSTRATION 10 Aron "incorporation of other into self" (IOS) scale by vignette condition

post-hoc analysis showed that the level of POSEMO allocated to the female agentic (FA) character does not differ significantly from the level of POSEMO given the male communal (MC) character. The discussion of this data pattern is expanded below.

4 Conclusions

In summary, measuring the social approval a subject displayed toward a central vignette character explicitly using the IOS measuring instrument, showed

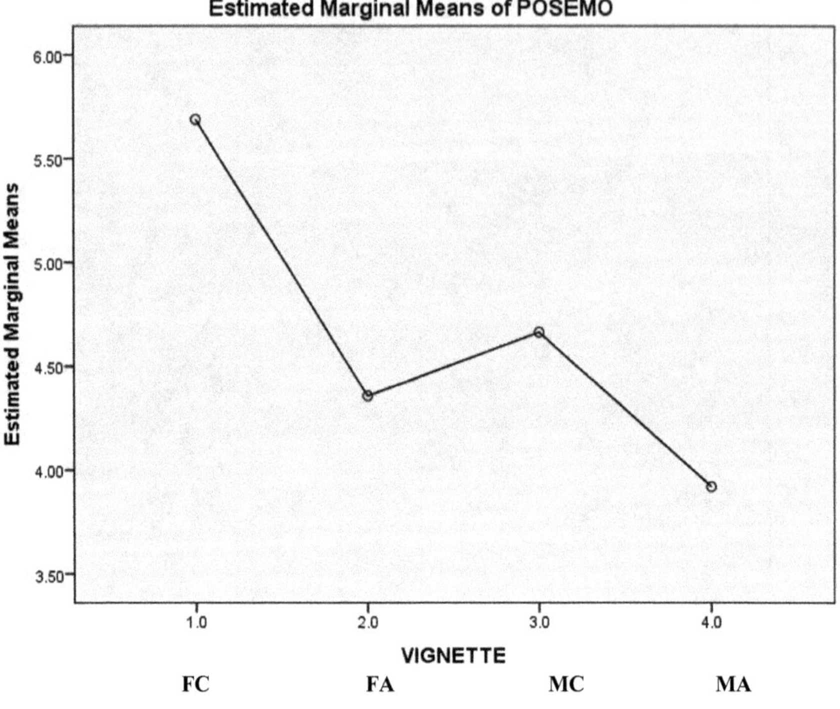

FC **FA** **MC** **MA**

FC = female-communal (*SD*

1.30*) FA = female-agentic (*SD

***1.85*) MC = male-communal**

(*SD 1.56*) MA = male-agentic

(*SD* 1.55)

ILLUSTRATION 11 LIWC "positive emotion-word use" (POSEMO) by vignette condition

no effect of gender variation. This finding supports the logic of MODE THEORY as an interpretation of "social desirability response bias." In light of these data, it seems highly plausible that that the explicit measuring instrument used in this study encouraged subjects to engage in controlled, deliberate cognitive processing, constructing a judgment to fit wider cultural/normative expectations surrounding and governing the situation. That is, use of the explicit measure of social approval led to subjects displaying a "socially desirable" attitude. Underlying such an attitude display is conformity with widely held cultural norms stipulating that, within the vignette-mediated quandary, selfless family affection should unambiguously take precedence over the self-interested pursuit of money. Motivated to convey such a self-impression, a subject should and did appear to hold gender to be completely irrelevant.

By contrast, measuring the social approval a subject displayed toward a central vignette character implicitly using the LIWC/POSEMO measuring instrument, showed a significant, nuanced effect of the gender-stereotype. This finding also supports the logic of MODE theory. It seems plausible that use of this alternative measure allowed for and encouraged spontaneous-automatic judgments in the subjects. The operation of these nuanced, gender-biased expectations can be seen in Illustration 11. A female central character making a decision based entirely on selfless family affection is provided a substantial "bonus" in POSEMO, compared with a male central character also making a decision based entirely on selfless family affection. Indeed, the male central character is granted no more POSEMO than the female central character who makes a decision based entirely on the self-interested pursuit of money. Further in line with the pervasive gender stereotype, the male central character making a decision based on the self-interested pursuit of money is allocated the lowest level of POSEMO of all characters depicted in the vignettes.

To elaborate the results briefly, it is worth noting that the explicit measuring instrument (IOS) uses a highly structured, "forced-choice" format. It is consistent with MODE theory to argue that this format itself creates an opportunity for deliberate-controlled cognitive processing of the situation: a subject reads a vignette and considers how close to or distant from a central character she/he should place her/himself. The Venn-diagram technique at the heart of the scale is geo-spatial in nature. The task facing the subject is an inherently analytical problem requiring the use of "higher order" reasoning. The subject is likely to employ conscious, explicit cognitive assets in such analysis. In effect, the subject might well ask: "As a member of the broader community, should I identify with a central character like this, and, if so, how much?" The data pattern shown in Figure 1 seems likely, given such deliberate-controlled cognitive processing. A subject might well reason: "In this vignette situation, where the needs of a disabled elderly parent should be considered paramount, a socially desirable reaction requires the gender of the central character be considered irrelevant: and all that should really matter is that altruistic family affection underlies the central character's decision regarding the elderly, afflicted parent."

By contrast, the LIWC psycholinguistic tool used to measure POSEMO in the present study, in part, allowed a relatively unstructured, open-ended response. Again, consistent with the logic of MODE theory, this measurement format provides an unfettered opportunity for spontaneous-automatic cognitive processing of the situation: A subject reads a vignette and is asked to write an open-ended essay imaginatively describing the central character's life (family, work, friendship, religion, politics, civic activity, and recreation). Constructing such a description in writing is an *explicit focus* of the task facing the subject, a focus that no doubt evokes as much deliberate-controlled cognitive processing as that evoked by the forced-choice IOS Venn- diagram task. On the one hand, a subject's explicit attention is deflected toward building an account of various domains in the central character's life. Simultaneously on the other hand, however, the LIWC POSEMO writing task provides a subject the opportunity for spontaneous- automatic responding in the form of an unstructured, open-ended choice of words to capture various facets of the central character's life. It seems plausible to construe this facet of cognitive processing as a quick, spontaneous, automatic and largely unconscious display by subjects of gender biases in reference to the central character.

The results of the present study support Fazio's MODE theory linking measurement to social desirability response bias in the context of a vignette experiment. While these results are limited, they provide a foundation upon which future research can build.

One limitation derives from the size and character of the subject sample used in the present study. Future research should increase both the size and diversity of the subject sample. It is quite likely subject gender would interact with the gender variations across the vignettes in important ways, and such interactions require careful study. A potentially useful strategy would be to build theoretically and operationally from the present vignette experiment toward a more ambitious factorial survey. As noted above, the central goal of the present experiment has been to test an abstract, general theory (the MODE framework), and the internal validity of causal inference has been given primacy. However, future work might buttress the present results, using the more descriptive, more ecologically focused methods of the factorial survey. In short, it would be valuable to explore the relationship between measurement and social desirability response bias in larger, more representative samples drawn from varying populations. Such exploration would expand the scope of the present findings by adding greater external (ecological) validity to the results.

A second limitation of the present study is the scope of the normative/cultural context created by the vignette manipulation. While the context created in the present study has been a useful means for testing a key theoretical hypothesis, many other normative/cultural contexts might and should also be studied rigorously. Future research should expand the vignette-mediated motives underlying decision-making beyond the clash between "communion" vs. "agency" used in the present study. Also, subject characteristics other than gender (age, education, health, and socio-economic status, among others) should be studied. A major virtue of vignette methods is that they flexibly allow the investigation of a wide variety of traits and social situations to be used in defining culturally/normatively "sensitive" and "problematic" situations. This virtue should be capitalized on in the development of follow-up studies.

A third limitation of the present study is the scope of the indicators used to explicitly and implicitly measure self-reported attitude. To measure other relevant constructs explicitly, a large variety of direct, "forced choice" items and scales in addition to the IOS scale used in the present study might be developed or borrowed from previous research. To measure other relevant constructs implicitly, other indicators in addition to the LIWC/POSEMO indicator used in the present study might be employed. For example, the "implicit association test" (Greenwald and Banaji, 1995), and other derivative response latency measures, might be used. One would expect studies using different indicators, explicit or implicit, to yield results consistent with those found in the present research.

More broadly, as Evans et al. (2014) make clear, vignette research methodologies provide a rich, flexible toolkit for studying important, variegated topics in clinical and health psychology. Using these methodologies, however, demands that researchers take careful account of the core issue surrounding the potential impact of measurement strategy (explicit vs. implicit) on social desirability response bias. The results of the present study suggest one potentially important pathway to pursue in dealing effectively with this issue.

5 Summary

The study presented in this chapter can be briefly summarized as follows:

Experimental vignette research methods have been used to study a diverse range of theoretical and practical issues. Vignettes are designed to create hypothetical cultural/normative contexts for the study of variation in self-reported attitudes. A key problem in such research, however, is potential social desirability response bias. A vignette experimental test of an hypothesis derived from a dual-process theory (the MODE framework initially developed by Fazio) linking explicit vs. implicit self-reported attitude measurement and social desirability response bias was reported in this chapter. The data showed that measuring the social approval of a central vignette character *explicitly* resulted in greater social desirability responding than measuring such approval *implicitly*, supporting MODE theory. We concluded that vignette research methodologies provide a rich, flexible toolkit for studying many important social psychological topics, including issues stemming from structural power-dependence inequality across a wide variety of social settings and situations. However, we argued that researchers can and should design a measurement strategy that carefully manages inferences drawn in light of conditions likely to produce social desirability response bias.

References

Abele, A. & Wojciszke, B. (2007) Agency and communion from the perspective of self versus others. *Journal of Personality and Social Psychology* 93:751–763.

Aron, A., Aron, E., Tudor, M., & Nelson, G. (1991) Close relationships as including other in the self. *Journal of Personality and Social Psychology* 60:241–253.

Berry, J.M., Williams, H.L., Thomas, K.D., and Blair, J. (2015) Perceptions of competence: Age moderates views of healthy aging and Alzheimer's disease. *Experimental Aging Research* 41:157–176.

Chaiken, S. and Trope, Y. (1999) Dual-Process Theories in Social Psychology. New York: Guilford Press.

Davis, S. & Greenstein, T. (2009) Gender ideology: Components, predictors, and consequences. *Annual Review of Sociology* 35:87–105.

Eagly, A. (1987) Sex differences in social behavior: A social-role interpretation. Hillsdale, NJ: Erlbaum.

Evans, S.C., Roberts, M.C., Keeley, J.W., Blossom, J.B., Amaro, C.M., Garcia, A.M., Stough, C.O., Canter, K.S., Robles, R., and Reed, G.M. (2014) Vignette methodologies for studying clinicians' decision-making: Validity, utility, and application in ICD-11 field studies. *International Journal of Clinical and Health Psychology* 15:160–170.

Fazio, R.H. (1990) Multiple Processes by which attitudes guide behavior: The MODE model as an integrative framework. *Advances in Experimental Social Psychology* 23:75–109.

Fazio, R.H. and Olson, M.A. (2003) Implicit measures in social cognition research: Their meaning and use. *Annual Review of Psychology* 54:297–327.

Fitzgerald, C. and Hurst, S. (2017) Implicit bias in healthcare professionals: a systematic review. *BMC Medical Ethics* 18:1–18.

Greenwald, A. and Banaji, M. (1995) Implicit social cognition: Attitudes, self-esteem, and stereotypes. *Psychological Review* 102:4–27.

Guest, G. and Namey, E. (eds.) (2014) Public Health Research Methods. Beverly Hills, CA: Sage.

Kada, O. (2017) Hospital transfers of nursing home residents: A vignette experiment on nurses' decision-making. *Journal of Applied Gerontology* 1:1–11.

Pennebaker, J.W., Chung, C.K., Ireland, M., Gonzales, A., and Booth, R.J. (2007) The Development and Psychometric Properties of LIWC2007. Austin, TX: LIWC.net.

Remler, D.K. and Van Ryzin, G.G. (2015) Research Methods in Practice. Los Angeles: Sage.

Rossi, H. and Nock, S. (1982) Measuring social judgments: The factorial survey. Beverly Hills, CA: Sage.

Santoro, M.S., Van Liew, C., Holloway, B., McKinnon, S., Little, T. and Cronan, A. (2016). *Research on Aging* 38:665–688.

Stolte, J.F. (1994) The context of satisficing in vignette research. *Journal of Social Psychology* 134:727–733.

Stolte, J.F. & Fender, S. (2007) Framing social values: An experimental study of Culture and cognition. *Social Psychology Quarterly* 70:59–69.

Tausczik, Y. & Pennebaker, J. (2010) The psychological meaning of words: LIWC and computerized Text Analysis Methods. *Journal of Language and Social Psychology* 9:24–54.

Teti, A., Gross, C., Knoll, N., and Bluher, S. (2016) Feasibility of the factorial survey method in aging research: Consistency effects among older respondents. *Research on Aging* 38:715–741.

Zamir and Teichman (eds.) (2014) The Oxford Handbook of Behavioral Economics and the Law. Oxford University Press.

CHAPTER 5

Exploring the Relationship between Agency and Communion

1 Testing the "Primacy of Communion" Hypothesis

Abele and Wojciszke (2007;2014) provide a comprehensive, authoritative review and synthesis of many lines of social psychological research addressing the core importance and nature of Bakan's classic (1966) distinction between "agency" vs. "communion." Their review covers early and contemporary work on such topics as person perception, theories of personality, the basic psychological contrast between femininity vs. masculinity, psychological variations across cultures, and fundamental typologies of social motives.

Central to their synthesis is the "the Dual-Perspective Model" (DPM). This theoretical framework draws a critically important distinction between the perspective of one actor, Perceiver A, and the perspective of a second actor, Target B. Whether "agency" or "communion" has primacy depends upon which of these two perspectives is assumed in a given instance.

For example, imagine Perceiver A has recently moved into a new neighborhood within a new city. A's next-door neighbor, Target B, has resided in the neighborhood and city for a number of years and is very familiar with this residential environment. Suppose A and B serendipitously meet face-to-face for the first time at the neighborhood mailbox. Let us first place ourselves in Perceiver A's perspective, from which A appraises Target B. Does A appraise B as being warm, friendly, empathic, cooperative, and sincere? If so, A's experience of B is "*communal*," and A is likely to become oriented toward B as an approachable, trustworthy interaction partner at present and in future social encounters.

By contrast, let us alternatively place ourselves in the perspective of Target B. In this case, DPM argues that B's focus is the self. As Actor B directs perception and appraisal toward various qualities of the self, B seeks to see the self as confident, competent, smart, skilled, and leader-like? Within this perspective, B's experience of the self tends to be "*agentic*." B thinks about and feels toward the self as being efficacious, as being generally capable of pursuing and achieving various gratifying "success goals."

According to Abele and Wojciszke, it is important to distinguish and consider *both* of these two distinct perspectives. In short, if we are to understand

 | DOI:10.1163/9789004713918_006

the complex agency/communion dynamic, we must not limit the perspective we take exclusively to one actor, either A or B.

Much research guided by the DPM has supported the principle that communion has primacy over agency. A wide body of evidence shows that Perceiver A tends to find communal qualities in Target B across many varying contexts. As summarized by Abele and Wojciszke (2014: 214–216), research on language, on "human universals" operating across many cultures, on processing multiple kinds of information, and on "enlightened self-interest" (i.e., where actors have an active awareness of the importance of "other profitability" and "self-profitability") consistently show support for the "primacy of communion" hypothesis.

Among the key theoretical reasons to expect empirical support for this hypothesis are the basic exigencies of human evolution: it will be generally adaptive, if Perceiver A can and regularly does discern that Target B is trustworthy and potentially beneficial. If A detects "communal" traits in B, A can safely interact with B, comfortably obtaining generally positive, even essential, interaction outcomes at present and in the future. In the hypothetical example outlined above, if the new neighbor, A, perceives the experienced neighbor, B, as "communal," A can potentially gain access to valuable information about the neighborhood, for example when the daily mail is delivered, what day of the week the garbage is picked up, or the best near-by grocery store to shop at. Furthermore, a communal B might also become the source of many other kinds of useful information and rewarding opportunities: contacts with other influential people to whom B is connected, who might mediate various gratifying "success goals" for Perceiver A, from a new, better career position to better schools for A's children, to many other kinds of "success goal" opportunities.

However, according to the DPM other contrasting bodies of research show that while communion generally has primacy in social interaction, the second perspective takes precedence under some conditions. When this happens, Target B becomes oriented to the self and "agency" tends to operate. For example, as experienced neighbor B appraises the self, he/she seeks to discover confidence, assertiveness, competence, and effectiveness, all qualities likely to lead to various "success goals," including a relatively favorable neighborhood status, including visibility, attention, pride and social self-efficacy.

In light of the Dual-Perspective Model, and building upon Abele and Wojciszke's important work, the present study was designed to examine "agency-communion" dynamics, with special focus upon evaluating the central notion that "communion has primacy over agency."

2 Method

2.1 *Subjects*

After obtaining university IRB committee approval, in exchange for course credit, and after signing an informed consent form, N = 52 college student volunteers served as the experimental subjects.[1]

2.2 *Procedure*

A hypothetical social context was created by designing a set of four brief vignettes. This context involved a serious family problem: an adult child must decide how to provide care for an older parent suffering from severe early-onset Alzheimer's disease/dementia. Across all the vignettes, the adult child is designated as the central character. The central character must consider all relevant circumstances and then make a decision about how best to care for the frail parent. In one set of vignettes, the adult child and the impaired elderly parent are described as female (an adult daughter and her elderly mother). In another set of vignettes, the adult child and the disabled elderly parent are depicted as male (an adult son and his elderly father). In one set of vignettes, the *motive determining the caregiving decision* made by the central character (either the adult daughter or adult son) is "*communal*" (i.e., the stated motive clearly displays only selfless family affection). In another set of vignettes, the motive shaping the caregiving decision is "*agentic*" (i.e., the motive clearly reveals an obvious self-centered pursuit of a central "success goal," personal money-inheritance). We reasoned that the *decision-making motive* would be an important manipulated factor across the vignettes. It seems plausible theoretically that this factor represents an important kind of information to Perceiver A (the subject). It is likely to be construed as a significant feature of the depicted social context.

It was also reasonable to expect that the *gender context* would be an important manipulated factor across the vignettes. Gender has been studied widely in the agency-communion literature, as Able and Wojciszke, (2007; 2014) have shown. Evidence (e.g., studies of stereotyping) has linked feminine qualities to "communion" and masculine qualities to "agency:" generally, women are seen

1 Some experimental materials (i.e., the experimental vignettes and subjects' essays) developed for use in the study reported above in Chapter 4, are also used in the study reported here in Chapter 5. The total N of subjects who participated in the Chapter 4 study was 149. The responses of only a subset (N = 55) subjects in that study wrote personal essays, and of those, the responses of 3 subjects were randomly dropped from the analysis reported in this chapter so as to create equal Ns for the statistical tests that were conducted here.

as and expected to be "communal," while men are portrayed as and expected to be "agentic." Further, additional research (Davis, S. & Greenstein, T., 2009; Eagly, A., 1987) has documented that social approval tends to be bestowed on actors and social situations congruent with the pervasive gender stereotype and social disapproval tends to be given actors and social situations deviating from the stereotype.

2.3 *Study Protocol*

Following are the four experimentally manipulated vignettes which were randomly assigned across the 52 subjects:

2.3.1 Experimentally Manipulated Variables

2.3.1.1 *Vignette Condition 1: Female/Communal (FC)*

"Consider the following two people:

Young Female photo	Middle aged Female photo

These photos are of a daughter (first photo) and her mother (second photo).

Recently, the older woman's (the mother's) health and mind have begun to decline, because she has been diagnosed with early-onset Alzheimer's disease. Physicians have indicated that they expect the mother's dementia to worsen over time to the point where she will not recognize her daughter.

At the present time, the mother needs a lot of help and support with the basic activities of daily living ... eating, bathing, dressing, walking, round-the-clock supervision, etc. In light of her mother's plight, the daughter is considering what decisions to make.

After struggling with all the issues, the daughter finally decides to have her mother move into her own home, so that she (the daughter) can care directly for all her mother's needs.

The daughter is moved to make this decision mainly in light of her high personal regard for and strong devotion to her mother. The daughter knows this decision will make her own life substantially more burdensome than placing her mother in a skilled nursing facility, but the daughter places her mother's welfare above her own, and simply wants to express her great affection for her mother."

2.3.1.2 *Vignette Condition 2: Female/Agentic (FA)*

"Consider the following two people:

Young Female photo	Middle Aged Female photo

These photos are of a daughter (first photo) and her mother (second photo).

Recently, the older woman's (the mother's) health and mind have begun to decline, because she has been diagnosed with early-onset Alzheimer's disease. Physicians have indicated that they expect the mother's dementia to worsen over time to the point where she will not recognize her daughter.

At the present time, the mother needs a lot of help and support with the basic activities of daily living … eating, bathing, dressing, walking, round-the-clock supervision, etc. In light of her mother's plight, the daughter is considering what decisions to make.

After struggling with all the issues, the daughter finally decides to have her mother move into her own home, so that she (the daughter) can care directly for all her mother's needs. The daughter is moved to make this decision mainly in light of practical economic circumstances.

The daughter knows that this decision will cost much less than placing her mother in a skilled nursing facility, and the daughter strongly wants to conserve her mother's wealth, so that when the mother dies, her (the daughter's) inheritance will be much greater than it would be otherwise."

2.3.1.3 *Vignette Condition 3: Male/Communal* (MC)

"Consider the following two people:

Young Male photo	Middle aged Male photo

These photos are of a son (first photo) and his father (second photo).

Recently, the older man's (the father's) health and mind have begun to decline, because he has been diagnosed with early-onset Alzheimer's disease. Physicians have indicated that they expect the father's dementia to worsen over time to the point where he will not recognize his son.

At the present time, the father needs a lot of help and support with the basic activities of daily living … eating, bathing, dressing, walking, round-the-clock supervision, etc. In light of his father's plight, the son is considering what decisions to make.

After struggling with all the issues, the son finally decides to have his father move into his own home, so that he (the son) can care directly for all his father's needs. The son is moved to make this decision mainly in light of his high personal regard for and strong devotion to his father. The son knows this decision will make his own life substantially more burdensome than placing his father in a skilled nursing facility, but the son places his father's welfare above his own, and simply wants to express his great affection for his father."

2.3.1.4 *Vignette Condition 4: Male/Agentic* (MA)
"Consider the following two people:

Young Male photo	Middle Aged Male photo

These photos are of a son (first photo) and his father (second photo).

Recently, the older man's (the father's) health and mind have begun to decline, because he has been diagnosed with early-onset Alzheimer's disease. Physicians have indicated that they expect the father's dementia to worsen over time to the point where he will not recognize his son.

At the present time, the father needs a lot of help and support with the basic activities of daily living … eating, bathing, dressing, walking, round-the-clock supervision, etc. In light of his father's plight, the son is considering what decisions to make.

After struggling with all the issues, the son finally decides to have his father move into his own home, so that he (the son) can care directly for all his father's needs. The son is moved to make this decision mainly in light of practical economic circumstances. The son knows that this decision will cost much less than placing his father in a skilled nursing facility, and the son strongly wants to conserve his father's wealth, so that when the father dies, his (the son's) inheritance will be much greater than it would be otherwise."

2.3.2 Dependent Variable

In light of DPM, each experimental subject can be considered *perceiver A*, while the hypothetical central character (adult child, daughter or son) described in the vignette can be construed as *Target B*.

As described above, one manipulated factor is the *central character's action decision motive*. The vignettes draw a clear contrast between being motivated exclusively by self-less family affection (construed here as a strong "communal" trait) and a practical, instrumental self-centered material focus on personal money-inheritance (taken here as a core "agentic" trait). As discussed above, the second manipulated factor is the *central character's gender*. Drawing from the DPM synthesis we expected that the effect of the action decision motive would be augmented by the stereotypical influence of gender: we expected that the female character would be viewed implicitly as being relatively more "communal," while the male character would be seen implicitly as being relatively more "agentic."

Deriving from the DPM synthesis, we reasoned that the *implicit motive to affiliate with the central character* would be a key dependent variable. Specifically, we followed Schultheiss (2013) in selecting the Linguistic Inquiry and Word Count program as a useful tool for measuring this variable. We reasoned that a relatively higher implicit motive to affiliate would signal Perceiver A's unconscious assessment that Target B is relatively trustworthy, safe, and socially approachable. The present study used the latest version of the Linguistic Inquiry and Word Count program, LIWC-22 (Boyd, R.L., Ashokkumar, A. and Francis, M.E., Pennebaker, J.W. 2022) for this measurement. LIWC analyzed and reported the proportion of words in the essays written by subjects as a reflection of the implicit motive to affiliate with the vignette central character.

In reference to the essays written by the 52 subjects, the specific experimental instructions were as follows: "In reference to the person shown in the first photo above (the younger person), please write a 250–350-word essay describing what you imagine that person's family, work, friendship, religion, politics, civic activity, and recreation are like."

2.3.3 Predictions following from the DPM Model

Effect of Central Character Decision Motive:

1. Perceiver A's (the subject's) implicit motive to affiliate will be greater in reference to the MC (male, communal) than the FA (female agentic) character.
2. Perceiver A's (the subject's) implicit motive to affiliate will be greater in reference to the FC (female communal) than the MA (male agentic) character.

Effect of Gender Context:

3. The effects of the central character's decision motive on the implicit motive to affiliate underlying hypotheses 1 and 2 above will be greater for the female than the male central characters.

2.4 *Results*

The first prediction was supported: Illustration 12 shows the pattern of implicit motive to affiliate with the central character depicted in each of the vignette conditions. As is seen in this Figure, the implicit motive to affiliate is significantly greater for MC (male communal character) than FA (female agentic character) (MC mean = 6.38, SD = 1.922, n = 13; FA mean = 4.95, SD = 1.36, n = 13).

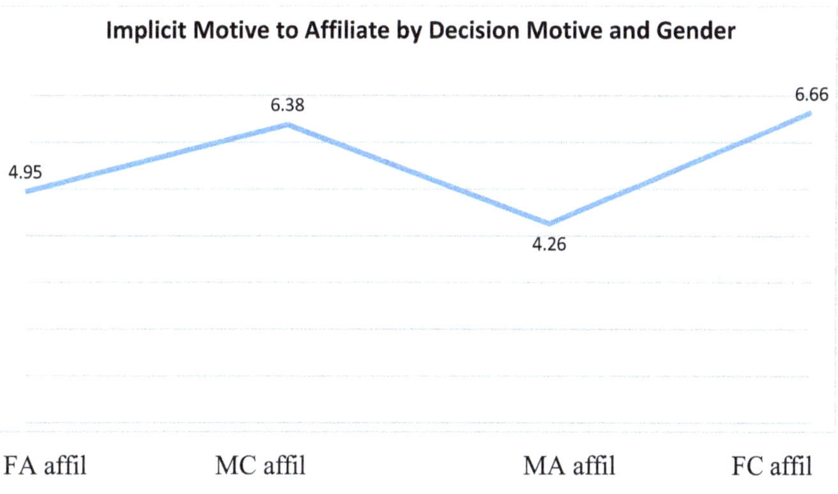

ILLUSTRATION 12 Implicit Motive to Affiliate by Decision Motive and Gender

The second prediction was also supported: as shown in Illustration 12, the implicit motive to affiliate was greater for FC (female communal character) than MA (male agentic character) (FC mean = 6.66, SD = 1.922, n = 13; MA mean = 4.26, SD = 1.60, n = 13). However, contrary to expectation, the third prediction was not supported: there was *no effect of the central character gender*: no significant differences were detected.

2.5 *Discussion of the Results*

In part, the data clearly support the DPM "primacy of communion" hypothesis. Specifically, the strong, consistent finding that an explicit communal decision motive shown by the central vignette character led to a significant increase among subjects in the *implicit motive to affiliate* with that central character. Other data gathered but not reported here (which are available from the author upon request) also seem relevant to and congruent with this hypothesis. In particular, one major thematic quality of social context conveyed explicitly across the vignettes was the quality, "*family*," expected to be a key determinant of a communal response in the subjects. As expected, the implicit reaction by the subjects to this quality was clear: they used significantly more "family" words in reference to the FC and MC vignettes, than the FA and MA vignettes. In short, subjects' implicit/unconscious responses paralleled the explicit/objective context provided by the vignettes regarding the context characteristic, "family."

Another part of the data seems to further support the "primacy of communion hypothesis." The FA and MA vignette central characters were designed to explicitly signal a self-centered concern with personal money-inheritance. The aim was explicitly to introduce a clash between this self-centered concern and the naturally "communal" context requiring a decision on how best to care for a frail, aging family member. The LIWC-22 analyses did show that the subjects implicitly recognized and responded to this explicit vignette-mediated theme of "*money-inheritance*": they used significantly more words connoting money in reference to those vignettes than they did in reference to the FC and MC vignettes. Interestingly, however, despite the theoretical intention behind the design of the explicit money-inheritance (FA and MA) context, that context evoked neither a significantly higher level of implicit *negative emotion* nor a significantly higher level of implicit *negative tone* toward the FA and MA central characters. (The relevant data are not presented here, but are available from the author by request.)

These unexpected non-results, in regard to what we thought would be a clear "agency-enhancing" context, seem to suggest that the "communal" principle out-weighed the "agentic" principle in shaping subjects overall implicit responses to the vignettes. And we construe these results as further support for the "primacy of communion" principle.

Importantly, other data collected in the study do not neatly fit the "primacy of communion" principle. One point stands out: gender had no effect. The motive to affiliate with the male Target B was just as high and not significantly different from the motive to affiliate with the female Target B. Evidently, the context created by the vignettes did not activate the Male-Female stereotype, did not activate the implicit gender bias we expected. Specifically, the prediction that subjects would express a significantly higher implicit motive to affiliate with the FC character than the MC character was not supported.

In sum, the vignettes stimulated a significantly stronger implicit motive to affiliate with central characters depicted as "communal" (FC and MC) than central characters depicted as "agentic" (FA and MA). However, contrary to expectation, gender did not amplify this effect, as predicted. Also, while a self-serving concern with personal money-inheritance was conveyed explicitly by the vignettes and implicitly recognized by the subjects, contrary to expectation, it did not evoke negative feelings among the subjects toward the vignette characters evincing this self-serving materialistic concern. We conclude, therefore, that the data reported here provide *strong but mixed support* for the hypothesis that "communion has primacy over agency," as suggested by the Dual Perspective Model. Complicating factors appear to have been at work determining subjects overall responses to the contexts established by the vignettes. We conclude that DPM is an important starting point, but that this model can and should be theoretically extended and refined.

Parenthetically, it should be noted that the DPM authors themselves have recently collaborated with other scholars within psychology to explore how their model might be elaborated and modified (Abele, Ellemers, Fiske, Koch, and Yzerbyt, 2021). We applaud their effort, because it underscores the importance of scholarly collaboration, debate, and refinement of any and all lines of research. We would add that it may also be useful to examine the communion-agency dynamic between psychology and sociology. In the spirit of expanding and refining ideas through interdisciplinary debate, we offer the following analysis.

2.5.1 Questions

In what specific directions would it be useful to expand the Dual Perspective Model of "agency" and "communion?" How might we clarify the conditions under which "communion" does indeed have primacy over "agency," but also perhaps alternative conditions under which "agency" has primacy over "communion?" Building upon the experimental results presented above, we briefly consider several pathways along which these questions might be examined.

2.5.2 Further Theoretical Exploration

Let us start by re-considering a central focus of DPM, the two perspectives of Perceiver A and Target B. This view might be expanded in two important ways. First, focus might shift to the reciprocal, mutual interactive relationship between two actors, A and B. That is, theoretical focus might *simultaneously consider* Perceiver A's orientation to Target B, as well as Perceiver B's orientation to Target A. Considering the longitudinal *interactive relationship* between A and B moves the "communion-agency" dynamic from within the psychology of an individual actor to the mutual social psychological relationship between two or possibly more actors. (An important general framework for moving in this direction is structural power-dependence theory.)

Second, theoretical focus might shift explicitly to consider the complex wider social world surrounding and impinging upon actors A and B. Such a shift of theoretical focus would prompt the analysis of linkages among the individual, relational, micro-collective, and macro-collective levels. Perhaps new, important insights would emerge by considering the effects of this wider social world on the communion-agency dynamic that unfolds between actors A and B. (Bringing in ideas concerning a surrounding, complex social exchange network might be useful.)

To pursue this proposed shift in theoretical focus, some core ideas will be drawn from three specific lines of social psychological work below. The first line of work bridges structural power-dependence social exchange theory

(Emerson, 1962; 1969; 1972; 1976; 1981) with symbolic interaction theory (Stolte, 1987b; Stolte, 1978b; Stolte, Fine, Cook, 2001). The second line of work deals with the process of socio-cultural framing (Goffman, 1974; Stolte and Fender, 2007). And, finally, the third line of work addresses the social psychology of "grappling," or "struggling" to make behavioral decisions in the face of existential dilemmas encountered within complex, ambiguous, often inconsistent socio-cultural situations that often arise in everyday social life (Fazio, 1990; Chaiken and Trope, 1999; Fazio and Olson, 2003; Stolte and Fender, 2007).

2.5.3 Distributive Exchange Networks, Productive Exchange Groups, and the Formation of Social Norms

As argued throughout this monograph, Emerson's structural power-dependence/social exchange network approach might well provide crucial insights into the dynamics of an interpersonal relationship between actors A and B. For example, actor A, implicitly or explicitly, at present or in the future, may become competitively self-interested in pursuing scarce, valued resources of all kinds that are potentially mediated by actor B, and vice versa. Within such a relationship, across time and transactions, A's gains in positive resource outcomes may result in B's loses, and/or vice versa. (See Stolte 1987a; 1990 for some of the relevant literature on power-dependence inequality and social stratification). In certain contexts, *resource distribution/competition* is the paramount quality characterizing the A-B relationship. Under this condition, each actor is likely to resist giving up costly, valuable resources. Likewise, each actor may be motivated to overcome such resistance in the other attempting to gain desired resources. Power-dependence, determined by relative resource value and resource availability, will determine the outcomes of such interpersonal competition/distribution and therefore whose benefits increase and whose benefits decrease correspondingly across time and transactions within the relationship.

Second, and expanding the view, power-dependence/exchange relations may become configured in larger, more complex structures ... social exchange networks... of varying configuration, and the relative position an actor occupies in such networks may be a crucial determinant of relative power advantage or disadvantage experienced by actors. Positional power as a causal factor in social exchange networks has been demonstrated to operate at a more complex structural level than power processes operating at the level of two-party A-B power-dependence/exchange relationship (Stolte and Emerson, 1977). The main point for the present analysis is that if such distributive/competitive issues are a significant property of a given relationship between actors A and

B, *"agency" is likely to have primacy over "communion,"* implicitly or explicitly, as both actors interact.

On the other hand, and importantly, power-dependence/social exchange relations and network structures are not limited to competitive resource distribution. As Emerson (1972) argued theoretically and Stolte (1987a) showed experimentally, sometimes a power-dependence/social exchange relationship between actors A and B entails exigencies of *production/cooperation.* In this case, two (or more) actors discover that their mutual best resource outcomes demand that they work together, that they "divide the labor" (Durkheim, 1893) in order to successfully resolve a common problem/task. In fact, the objective structural circumstance may dictate that neither A nor B (nor other actors) will realize a benefit unless they (all) cooperate and share the resulting valued resource outcomes. Where actors must collaboratively cooperate, their respective behavioral in-puts must be combined, coordinated, organized, and collectively enacted before either (any) actor will obtain a positive resource outcome ("positive success goal" in DPM terms). This second sort of exchange structural scenario, where the exigency of production/cooperation prevails, is likely to cause *"communion" to have primacy over "agency" for each actor in relation to all other actors.* Parenthetically, Emerson's (1972) distinction between distributive/competitive and productive/cooperative exchange is a strictly value-free part of an empirical behavioral theory. However, it can be conceptually linked to a classic, earlier debate in sociology between proponents of "functionalism" and proponents of "conflict theory" (Davis and Moore, 1945; Tumin, 1953; Wrong, 1961). Importantly, some contributions to that debate are not objective, scientific, and value-free, but rather are ideological.

As shown in Chapter 2 above, Emerson's structural power-dependence theory can be expanded by linking it with symbolic interaction theory (Stolte, 1987b; Stolte, Fine, and Cook, 2001). Cultural norms (including various morally legitimate norms of "justice") can form among actors who join together (productively/cooperatively) as members of social coalitions (organized groups). Through multi-party social negotiations, implicit or explicit, individual actors can coalesce in sharing meaning agreements. Multiple parties can, through this process, come to share ideas about what (objectively) "is" and about what (legitimately) "ought" to be true. Once formed, a social coalitional group is characterized by a shared agreement on principles that need to be enacted mutually by all coalition/group members. Such agreed upon principles, implicitly or explicitly, become social norms backed mutually by all coalitional/group actors in support of behavioral sanctioning. The result is individual action that conforms to shared social norms.

Individual social actors, from birth to death, as they go through life within the socio- cultural structure of social exchange are actively socialized by significant others. Often, they internalize social norms (Stolte, 1978b). Once internalized, norms may, implicitly or explicitly, become activated at given times under given social circumstances. What a given actor thinks, feels, and does at any given time and place is often governed by what that actor takes, implicitly or explicitly, to be an appropriate social norm. Some situations normatively dictate that "communion" be the basis of thinking, feeling, and action. Other situations normatively prescribe that "agency" underlie thinking, feeling, and action. Which of these fundamental principles has primacy at a given time in a given place depends upon how a given social situation becomes normatively instantiated and activated for social actors. This point brings us to the second line of work to be considered.

2.5.4 Social Situational and Social Value Framing

As argued throughout this monograph, to link structural power-dependence theory and symbolic interaction theory (Stolte1987b) implies that one point of view, based entirely on objective social behavior (social exchange), can and should explicitly be synthesized with another point of view which addresses subjective and inter-subjective social experience (symbolic interaction). Both perspectives considered together suggest that an actor is motivated to understand, implicitly and explicitly, the surrounding social situation and other actors who are present. An actor comes to grasp the meaning of the surrounding situation and other actors through a range of implicit and explicit language-based signs and symbols (Mead, 1934; Lindesmith and Strauss, 1950; Stryker, 2008). Some meanings emerge and form with reference to the surrounding external material conditions that constrain individual, interpersonal, and collective action opportunities and potential valued resource outcomes ("the is"). Other meanings emerge and form in reference to various internalized norms ("the ought").

As emphasized earlier in this monograph, an important dynamic through which situated meanings emerge is social framing (Goffman, 1974; Stolte and Fender, 2007). To effectively navigate a complex, changing, often inconsistent, socio-cultural setting composed of varying material conditions and varying social circumstances an actor must arrive at a workable social meaning (social frame) that governs that situation. In some instances, the relevant frame is distributive/competitive social exchange, while in other instances the relevant frame is productive/cooperative social exchange. In some cases, the relevant frame is set by a norm of "communion" (e.g., a situation involving family and friendship relations). In other cases, the relevant frame is set by a norm of "agency" (e.g., business and competitive market relations). A given actor, either individually or relationally in reference to other actors, must determine which social meaning framework applies within a given instance, time, and place. When it has emerged, a social frame governs the operative context of the situation at hand. Alone in communication with the self, or together in communication with other actors, an actor must engage, implicitly or explicitly, in symbolic interaction. That actor or actors must attend to and construe various language-based "cues," "messages," and "meanings" so as to establish a workable, relevant "definition of the situation" (Thomas, W.I. and Znaniecki, F., 1919).

We turn finally to a third line of work that might help expand understanding of the complex communion-agency dynamic.

2.5.5 Social Grappling

As noted earlier in this monograph, when navigating the complex sociocultural world, an actor often encounters ambiguities and inconsistencies. Arriving at a workable frame for a social situation often involves a social psychological process of "grappling." An actor frequently must struggle to answer emergent questions: What kind of material situation is at hand, distributive/competitive or productive/cooperative? How should the "cues" and "messages" emerging within the social situation be construed? Can and should an emerging meaning be, implicitly or explicitly, socially negotiated with other actors? What social norms appear valid and proper within the boundaries of the emergent social situation? Is the emergent situational frame "communal" or "agentic?"

To engage in social psychological grappling entails *dual cognitive processing* (Zajonc, 1980; Fazio, 1990; Chaiken and Trope, 1999; Metcalf and Mischel, 1999; Fazio and Olson, 2003; Lieberman, Jarcho, Sapute, 2004; Evans, 2008;) Under some conditions an actor will respond to situational "cues" or "messages" at a lower, "hot," automatic, implicit cognitive level. In this case, the actor unconsciously and impulsively responds, often through simplistic, vague, over-generalized stereotypes. Under other conditions, an actor responds to situational "cues" or "messages" at a higher, "cool," deliberative, explicit cognitive level. Here, the actor carefully, thoughtfully responds, attempting to be objective, logical, and rational. As a complex cognitive dynamic, social grappling often involves repeatedly shifting from a lower-implicit to higher-explicit level and from higher-explicit to lower-implicit level of processing across the unfolding social situation.

2.5.6 Brief Re-consideration of the Vignette Experimental Results

In light of the above theoretical exploration, we return briefly to the results of the vignette experiment. The subject is actor A, and the central vignette character is actor B. The experimental task facing a subject is to explicitly consider and appraise various features of the central character's life. From the essays written by subjects, LIWC-22 finds the implicit meanings arrived at by the subject. The entire scenario is couched in language processing, symbolic interaction. Vignettes explicitly presenting the central character as communal aroused the implicit motive to affiliate with the central character. Vignettes explicitly presenting the central as one gender or the other had no effect. Vignettes explicitly presenting a self-centered focus on money-inheritance did not produce implicit negative affect.

Our interpretation is that the vignettes brought to bear a wider socio-cultural context, required the subjects to settle on an apparently valid social frame, and required social grappling by the subjects so as to achieve that social frame. Part of the situation was explicit (each vignette was presented in formal writing under formal experimental instructions). Subjects' interpretations were governed partly by the formally written narrative. However, part of the situation was implicit: a subject had to fashion an appraisal of the vignette central character. To achieve an implicit valid and proper sense of the emergent and operative social frame (definition of the situation), a subject likely engaged in dual cognitive processing. In the end, all things considered, a subject framed the social situation with a well-internalized social norm: a hypothetical internal conversation with oneself might have gone something like this: "when family is involved, one should help, even at great self-sacrifice. To do so is expected by others and oneself. Gender should not matter! It is irrelevant. Also, why feel negative toward the FA and MA characters? It is easy to see and understand their situation. Like it or not, in the long- run, within the world as it is, money-inheritance does matter! Indeed, maybe the quality of care one can provide to a frail, disabled parent requires a significant amount of money."

3 Conclusion

The Dual Perspective Model is a valuable step toward understanding the communion-agency dynamic. Hopefully, the experimental results and exploratory theoretical ideas reported above will help expand thinking as well as spur additional empirical research. Gaining additional understanding of the varying conditions under which the "communal" principle and/or the "agentic" principle have primacy is a central task facing social psychology today and beyond.

4 Summary

In this chapter, the results of a vignette experiment supporting the "primacy of communion over agency" hypothesis implied by "the dual-perspective model" (Abele and Wojciszke, 2014) were reported. However, while we showed that the results partially support this model, they do not fit it completely and those results have prompted a wider exploration of some additional theoretical questions concerning the context, process, and outcomes of the communion-agency dynamic. The research reported in this chapter used the latest Linguistic Inquiry Word Count tool (LIWC-22) to analyze the implicit motive to affiliate observed in written transcripts collected as part of an earlier vignette experiment (the study by Stolte reported above in Chapter 4). The broad goal of the work reported in the present chapter has been to extend our grasp of the agency-communion dynamic as it operates across a wide array of social behavior and social situations. We (a) discussed the central logic of the "dual-perspective model" (DPM), (b) reported data partially supporting the "primacy of communion" hypothesis, then (c) expanded the analysis by examining three theoretical issue areas focused on: (i) the broader socio-cultural context, (ii) the interactive process of social framing, and (iii) the existential need for social grappling. We argued that while communion does, under certain conditions, have primacy over agency as DPM asserts, other conditions are likely to lead to the primacy of agency over communion. We argued that such other conditions need to be more fully explored and specified as theoretical scope conditions. We argued that structural power-dependence theory is a useful framework for doing so.

References

Abele, A.E. and Wojciszke, B. (2007) Agency and communion from the perspective of self versus others. *Journal of Personality and Social Psychology* 93, 5:751–763.

Abele, A.E. and Wojciszke, B. (2014) Communal and agentic content in social cognition: A dual perspective model. *Advances in Experimental Social Psychology* 50:195–225.

Abele, A., Ellemers, N., Fiske, S., Koch, A., and Yzerbyt, V. (2021) Navigating the social world: Toward an integrated framework for evaluating self, individuals, and groups. *Psychological Review* 128, 2:290–314.

Bakan, D. (1966) The Duality of Human Existence. Reading, PA: Addison Wesley.

Boyd, R., Ashokkumar A., Seraj, J., and Pennebaker, J. (2022) The development and psychometric properties of LIWC-22. Pennebaker Conglomerate. Austin : University of Texas,. November.

Chaiken, S. and Trope, Y. (1999) Dual-Process Theories in Social Psychology. New York: Guilford Press.

Davis, K. and Moore, W. (1945) Some Principles of Social Stratification. University of Chicago Press.

Davis, S. & Greenstein, T. (2009) Gender ideology: Components, predictors, and consequences. *Annual Review of Sociology* 35:87–105.

Durkheim, E. (1893) The Division of Labor in Society. Free Press.

Eagly, A. (1987) Sex Differences in Social Behavior: A Social-role Interpretation. Hillsdale, NJ: Erlbaum.

Emerson, R.M. (1972) Exchange Theory, Part II: Exchange Relations and Networks. In J. Berger, M. Zelditch, and B. Anderson (eds.) Sociological Theories in Progress, Vol. 2, 3–87, Boston: Houghton-Mifflin.

Emerson, R.M. (1969) Operant Psychology and Exchange Theory. In R.L. Burgess and D. Bushell (eds.) The Experimental Analysis of Social Processes: Implications for a Behavioral Sociology, 42–69, New York: Columbia University Press.

Emerson, R.M. (1962) Power-Dependence Relations. *American Sociological Review* 27, 3:31–40.

Emerson, R.M. (1976) Social Exchange Theory. *Annual Review of Sociology* 51, 3:335–362.

Emerson, R.M. (1981) Social Exchange Theory. In M. Turner and R. Rosenberg (eds.) Social Psychology: Sociological Perspectives, 81–113. New York: Basic Books.

Evans, J.B. (2008) Dual-Processing Accounts of Reasoning, Judgment, and Social Cognition. *Annual Review of Psychology* 59, 4:255–78.

Fazio, R.H. (1990) Multiple Processes by which attitudes guide behavior: The MODE model as an integrative framework. *Advances in Experimental Social Psychology* 23:75–109.

Fazio, R.H. and Olson, M.A. (2003) Implicit measures in social cognition research: Their meaning and use. *Annual Review of Psychology* 54:297–327.

Goffman, E. (1974) Frame Analysis: An Essay on the Organization of Experience. Harvard University Press.

Lindesmith, A.R. and Strauss, A.L. (1950) A Critique of Culture-Personality Writings. *American Sociological Review* 15, 5:587–600.

Lieberman, M., Jarcho, J., and Satpute, A. (2004) Evidence-based and intuition-based self-knowledge: An fMRI study. *Journal of Personality and Social Psychology*, 421–435.

Mead, G.H. (1934) Mind, Self, and Society. Chicago: University of Chicago Press.

Metcalfe, J. and Mischel, W. (1999) A hot/cool-system analysis of delay of gratification: Dynamics of willpower. *Psychological Review* 106:3–19.

Schultheiss, O.C. (2013) Are implicit motives revealed in mere words? Testing the marker-word hypothesis with computer-based text analysis. *Frontiers in Psychology* 4:1–20.

Stolte, J.F. and Fender, S. (2007) Framing social values: An experimental study of culture and cognition. *Social Psychology Quarterly*, 59–69.

Stolte, J.F. and Emerson, R.M. (1977) Structural inequality: Position and power in network structures. In R. Hamblin and J. Kunkel (eds.) Behavioral Theory in Sociology: Essays in Honor of George C. Homans, 117–139. New Brunswick, NJ: Transaction.

Stolte, J.F., Fine, G., and Cook, K. (2001) Sociological miniaturism: Seeing the big through the small in social psychology. *Annual Review of Sociology* 27, 1:387–413.

Stolte, J.F. (1990) Power processes in structures of dependence and exchange. *Advances in Group Processes* 7:129–50.

Stolte, J.F. (1987a) Legitimacy, justice, and productive exchange. In K. Cook (ed.) Social Exchange Theory, Sage Publications.

Stolte, J.F. (1987b) The formation of justice norms. *American Sociological Review*, 774–784.

Stolte, J.F. (1978b) Internalization: A bargaining network approach. *Journal for the Theory of Social Behavior* 8, 3:297–312.

Stryker, S. (2008) From Mead to a structural symbolic interactionism and beyond. *Annual Review of Sociology* 34, 1:15–31.

Thomas, W.I. and Znaniecki, F. (1919) The Polish Peasant in Europe and America. University of Chicago Press.

Tumin, M. (1953) Some principles of stratification: A critical analysis. *American Sociological Review* 18, 4:387–394.

Wrong, D. (1961) The over-socialized conception of man in modern sociology. *American Sociological Review*, 183–193.

Zajonc, R.B. (1980) Feeling and thinking: Preferences need no inferences. *American Psychologist*, 151–175.

CHAPTER 6

Exploring Gender and Implicit Self-appraisal: Empirical Research Context

The research presented in this chapter, which uses the LIWC-22 tool for psycholinguistic analysis, is based on a corpus of personal writings drawn from a non-profit, publically available, online source: the Digital Archive of Literacy Narratives (https://www.thedaln.org/#/home), a site that has been accessible since 2007. This site was designed for teachers, students, and other writers to share personal self-appraisals of their experiences in mastering and using English for clear, competent, practical and/or creative writing.

From the DALN site, a convenience sample of personal essays (n = 85 written by females and n = 85 written by males) was selected. Average essay length was several Word document pages. Each essay was voluntarily posted by its author to this site. Each author who posted an essay could choose whether or not to self-identify or remain anonymous. The present study selected both self-identified and anonymous essays for analysis. However, all authors whose essays have been used will remain anonymized.[1] Only aggregated statistical results and a theoretical interpretation are presented here.

We used LIWC-22 (Boyd, et al. 2022) to conduct a psycholinguistic study of this corpus of writings. Below the basic results of this study are presented.

1 Gender Differences

The LIWC-22 Data display the following results:

a. Females show a significantly higher level of *implicit "social reference"* than Males. (F mean = 5.86, M mean = 5.28); ($t = 1.63$; $p < .05$).
b. Females show a significantly higher level of *implicit "I-talk"* than Males. (F mean = 8.32, M mean = 7.98) ($t = 0.83$; $p < .05$).
c. Females show a significantly higher level of *implicit "want"* than Males. (F mean = 0.34, M mean = 0.25) ($t = 1.65$; $p < .05$).

1 See Weinhardt, 2020, for a recent, authoritative discussion of the ethical issues surrounding the use of online data for social research.

 | DOI:10.1163/9789004713918_007

2 Proposed Theoretical Account of These Results

We can tentatively but plausibly account for these findings by drawing together several lines of social psychological research and theory.

Consider the first finding above. In the context of appraising oneself in relation to mastering literacy, the implicit salience of *"social reference"* is aroused more strongly in females than males. This finding, of course, is no surprise given the long-standing body of research findings by many gender researchers (including Eagly, 1987; Davis and Greenstein, 2009; Myers-Lev and Loken, 2015; Eagly and Scezesny, 2019). Many studies across varying settings, at the macro, meso, and micro levels of analysis, across history and modern society have shown (and still show) that females tend to display behavioral qualities characterized as socially connected, outreaching, interdependent, nurturing, communicative. That is, females are typically found to pour themselves into building and maintaining solid, lasting *communal* bonds (e.g., marriage, family, close friendship circles.) By contrast, the research has shown that males tend toward being relatively more socially distant/separate, generally more socially independent. That is, male behavioral qualities lean toward effective individual *agency* in the competitive pursuit of greater power, status, and achievement (work, income, material status.)

Consider the second finding above. In this context of literacy self-appraisal, females show a significantly stronger tendency to *use the personal pronoun, "I" (engage in more "I-talk")* than males. This language behavior clearly suggests that females implicitly grasp a traditional, structural, cultural position that is *lower* in the broad power/status hierarchy relative to males. Research results by Kacewicz et al., 2013 and Berry-Blunt, et al. 2021 strongly support this interpretation.

As Berry-Blunt et al. (2021) note, those who use "I" less frequently (males in the present study) tend to be: "more emotionally stable", "acquisitive," "powerful" "esteemed," "less open-minded," "more confident and resolute." By contrast, those who more frequently use I-talk (females in the present research) tend to be "more emotionally vulnerable," "resentful," "report more depressive symptoms," "seem more preoccupied."

At a broad, general level, these findings fit theory/research focused on links among: structural power-dependence and social exchange, symbolic interaction, and socio-cultural framing (as the foregoing chapters of the present monograph have argued and shown). In short, it is reasonable to conclude that females have a strong implicit grasp of occupying a generally power-disadvantaged position relative to males, who have traditionally and generally used their power-advantage to obtain a relatively greater share of many kinds of valuable (extrinsic/agentic) resources (e.g., better jobs, more money, more prominence/prestige/social influence across many kinds of social situations). Moreover, the findings suggest that, in response, females implicitly react as one would reasonably predict: on the one hand, they are frustrated, depressed, resentful, and emotionally vulnerable; but, on the other hand (as argued below), they are implicitly open and ready to mobilize action aimed at changing the opportunity structure so as to get a greater share of extrinsic/agentic outcomes traditionally dominated by males. Women are implicitly ready to work toward balancing the historically anchored and currently operative imbalanced power structure that has here-to-fore favored males.

Consider the third finding above. In this research context of self-appraised literacy mastery, females showed significantly greater implicit "want" than males. This finding requires a nuanced, multi-pronged interpretation in light of past research on (a) dual-processing (Zajonc, 1980; Fazio, 1990; Chaiken and Trope, 1999; Metcalf and Mischel, 1999; Fazio and Olson, 2003; Lieberman, Jarcho, Sapute, 2004; Evans, 2008), (b) the "should self" vs. the "want self," (Simola, 2017; Williams, 2023) and, (c) implicit/explicit "grappling" with the complexities of pluralistic, often inconsistent, social frames that constantly emerge and rapidly change in everyday social life (see earlier chapters in the present monograph on this point).

It is plausible, in the present research context, that females do not feel completely limited to an implicit "should-want" system anchored in the past. That is, females do not willingly accept, as their exclusive or even central social role arena, the dutiful fulfillment of the communal expectations socially imposed by history and society upon them. They do not subscribe to a norm that has traditionally narrowed their legitimate pursuits to building and maintaining strong social communal bonds (e.g., becoming and remaining first and foremost good wives, mothers, and friends). The data suggest, instead, that they do not feel it is proper to always be implicitly pushed to take a "back seat" to males in the competition for greater success in the attainment of extrinsic/agentic resources. Instead, the females in the present study seem to exhibit a significant implicit "self-want." We construe this exhibited implicit "want" as thoroughly instrumental: females want to master literacy, perhaps because literacy is a profoundly useful tool-set required to make real, substantial gains in upward social/material mobility. If successful in mastering literacy, females implicitly sense that balancing power in relation to males is substantially more likely. Being confident and competent in the realm of literacy, perhaps they implicitly sense, would likely facilitate access to leadership roles, more influential organizational positions, higher income, and more social attention/prestige/influence. In short, we argue here that the (self) "wanting" exhibited by females relative to males in the present findings implicitly promises greater potential success within the extrinsic/agentic opportunity structures previously and currently dominated by males.

Parenthetically, a broader informational backdrop for the current research findings seems relevant. Perhaps the females in the current sample are at least vaguely aware of the long-existing fact that females typically excel over males in regard to language/reading mastery. This fact is solidly supported by much research (Reilly, et al., 2019), and is widely known by the general public. Are the females studied here implicitly aware that they have a distinct advantage relative to males specifically in the area of literacy? If so, does such implicit awareness activate and motivate a growing sense of self-efficacy in females as they actively strive for power/status gains in their competition with males? Affirmative answers to these questions, go beyond the data presented here. But, in the larger context of theory, research, and common sense, they seem plausible.

3 Conclusion

Clearly, the present research is far from definitive. Much more work needs to be done. For example, the findings reported here ought to be buttressed by studies using other methods besides LIWC linguistic analysis of implicit responses. For example, factorial surveys using experimental vignettes designed to tap both explicit and implicit cognitions, motives, and actions would be a promising general avenue to pursue in further research. Using such methodology could further illuminate in the study of gender differences. Such an approach could promote substantially greater optimization of internal and external validity of results, not attainable by the non-experimental, correlational approach and convenience sampling approach used in the present report.

Other theoretical lines of work, besides exchange theory, also should be leveraged, going forward. One promising direction, for example, is the study of "*ambivalence*" (see Luttrell, et al., 2016; Durso, et al., 2016). It seems reasonable, based on the present study, that females are generally quite ambivalent: certain contexts implicitly obligate the "*should-self*" of females, moving them to engage in strong exclusive pursuit of "*communal*" outcomes, while, simultaneously, other contexts implicitly compel the "*want-self*" moving them in the opposite direction of seeking to be effective in balancing power in the competition with males for various "*agentic*" outcomes. Studying exactly how females (and males) grapple with and resolve such likely pervasive ambivalence would be extremely informative in future studies.

Such follow-up work can and should extend the findings reported here, adding evidence and developing theory that can help clarify our grasp of the causes and consequences of gender differences in implicit self-appraisal, a topic of enduring importance. Using the structural power-dependence/social exchange framework can be useful in pursuing this continued line of research.

4 Summary

The study reported in this chapter was inductive, correlational, and exploratory. Rather than testing predictions derived logically from an extant theory, it used the Linguistic Inquiry and Word Count (LIWC-22) tool to empirically explore and interpret gender differences in implicit self-appraisal in a corpus of personal writings by females and males (n = 170). As noted above, the explicit context of these writings was self-appraised mastery of literacy (language, competent writing, creative analysis, and storytelling). In this research context, LIWC-22 disclosed three significant gender differences in implicit self-appraisal: females displayed higher levels of (a) "*social reference*" (b) "*I-talk*," and (c) "*want*," than males. Several lines of prior social psychological research were linked to offer a theoretical account of these findings. While post-hoc and tentative, this account seems plausible. Building from the structural power-dependence framework, the research presented in this chapter can and should be, further tested, questioned, extended, and refined to broaden our understanding of gender differences in implicit self-appraisal across varying social contexts.

References

Berry-Blunt, A., Holtzman, N., Donnellen, M., and Mehl, M. (2021) The story of "I-tracking": Psychological implications of self-referential language use. *Social and Personality Compass,* forthcoming, 1–36.

Boyd, R., Ashokkumar A., Seraj, J., and Pennebaker, J. (2022) The development and psychometric properties of LIWC-22. Pennebaker Conglomerates. Austin: University of Texas. November.

Chaiken, S. and Trope, Y. (1999) Dual-Process Theories in Social Psychology. New York: Guilford Press.

Davis, S. & Greenstein, T. (2009) Gender ideology: Components, predictors, and consequences. *Annual Review of Sociology* 35:87–105.

Durso, G., Brinol, P., and Petty, R. (2016) From power to inaction: Ambivalence gives pause to the powerful. *Psychological Science* 27:1660–1666.

Eagly, A. (1987) Sex Differences in Social Behavior: A Social-role Interpretation. Hillsdale, NJ: Erlbaum.

Eagly, A., and Sczesny, S. (2019) Editorial: gender roles in the future? Theoretical foundations and future research directions. *Frontiers in Psychology* 10:1–3.

Evans, J.B. (2008) Dual-Processing Accounts of Reasoning, Judgment, and Social Cognition. *Annual Review of Psychology* 59, 4:255–78.

Fazio, R.H. (1990) Multiple Processes by which attitudes guide behavior: The MODE model as an integrative framework. *Advances in Experimental Social Psychology* 23:75–109.

Fazio, R.H. and Olson, M.A. (2003) Implicit measures in social cognition research: Their meaning and use. *Annual Review of Psychology* 54:297–327.

Kacewicz, E., Pennebaker, J., Davis, M., Jeon, M., and Graesser, A. (2013) Pronoun use reflects standings in social hierarchies. *Journal of Language and Social Psychology* 10, 20:1–19.

Lieberman, M., Jarcho, J., and Satpute, A. (2004) Evidence-based and intuition-based self-knowledge: An fMRI study. *Journal of Personality and Social Psychology*, 421–435.

Luttrell, A., Petty, R., Brinol, P. (2016) Ambivalence and certainty can interact to predict attitude stability. *Journal of Experimental Social Psychology* 63:56–68.

Metcalfe, J. and Mischel, W. (1999) A hot/cool-system analysis of delay of gratification: Dynamics of willpower. *Psychological Review* 106:3–19.

Myers-Levy, J. and Lokan, B. (2015) Revisiting gender differences. *Journal of Consumer Psychology* 25:129–149.

Reilly, D., Neumann, D., and Andrews, G. (2019) Gender differences in reading and writing achievement: Evidence from the National Assessment of Educational Progress (NAEP). *American Psychologist* 74: 445–458.

Simola, S. (2017) Managing for academic integrity in higher education: Insights from behavioral ethics. *Scholarship of Teaching and Learning in Psychology* 3:43–57.

Stolte, J.F. and Fender, S. (2007) Framing social values: An experimental study of culture and cognition. *Social Psychology Quarterly*, 59–69.

Stolte, J.F. and Emerson, R.M. (1977) Structural inequality: Position and power in network structures. In R. Hamblin and J. Kunkel (eds.) Behavioral Theory in Sociology: Essays in Honor of George C. Homans, 117–139. New Brunswick, NJ: Transaction.

Stolte, J.F., Fine, G., and Cook, K. (2001) Sociological miniaturism: Seeing the big through the small in social psychology. *Annual Review of Sociology* 27, 1:387–413.

Stolte, J.F. (1990) Power processes in structures of dependence and exchange. *Advances in Group Processes* 7:129–50.

Stolte, J.F. (1987a) Legitimacy, justice, and productive exchange. In K. Cook (ed.) Social Exchange Theory, Sage Publications.

Stolte, J.F. (1987b) The formation of justice norms. *American Sociological Review*, 774–784.

Stolte, J.F. (1978) Internalization: A bargaining network approach. *Journal for the Theory of Social Behavior* 8, 3:297–312.

Stryker, S. (2008) From Mead to a structural symbolic interactionism and beyond. *Annual Review of Sociology* 34, 1:15–31.

Thomas, W.I. and Znaniecki, F. (1919) The Polish Peasant in Europe and America. University of Chicago Press.

Tumin, M. (1953) Some principles of stratification: A critical analysis. *American Sociological Review* 18, 4:387–394.

Weinhardt, M. (2020) Ethical issues in the use of big data for social research. *Historical Social Research* 45:342–368.

Williams, D. (2023) A meta-theoretical framework for organizing and integrating theory and research on motivation for health-related behavior. *Frontiers in Psychology* 23:1–10.

Wrong, D. (1961) The Over-socialized conception of man in modern sociology. *American Sociological Review*, 183–193.

Zajonc, R.B. (1980) Feeling and thinking: Preferences need no inferences. *American Psychologist*, 151–175.

PART 3

The Structural Power-Dependence Research Program: Assessment

∵

CHAPTER 7

Summary, Future Research Directions, and Conclusion

This monograph has discussed the nature of general process theories in the social sciences and has examined {Emerson's (1962;1969;1972) structural power-dependence formulation of social exchange networks in depth as an important instance of such a theory. The experiment by Stolte and Emerson (1977), inspired by Emerson's earlier theoretical work, was the first empirical study in the research program guided by the structural power-dependence framework. As the program of studies evolved, concepts, principles, and methods expanded beyond the basic methodological tenets of general process theory construction and the entirely objective operant-behavioral assumptions guiding Emerson's original exchange theory. New social psychological dimensions, research methods, and data were incorporated. The research direction broadened, and the cumulative results were enriched. A new aim had emerged: to systematically address issues of importance lying beyond the perimeter of the original exclusively objective behavioral formulation of social exchange networks. An early, important transition point was the explicit incorporation of concepts and assumptions drawn from symbolic interaction theory. With this transition, research focus shifted to links between subjective/intersubjective conditions and events, on the one hand, and objective/overt behavioral conditions and events, on the other hand. This shift of focus opened the program to considering important new topics of social exchange such as social norm formation, self-efficacy, agency vs. communion, and framing social situations and social values.

After reviewing previously published research in the program, the monograph reported a set of new, previously unpublished, studies. This new line of research displayed the continued evolution of the structural power-dependence research program. The new research shows the program's continued exploration and incorporation of new ideas and new research methods. First, a classic case study of the "Kula Ring," originally reported by Malinowski, was re-imagined to show how ethnography can illuminate and concretize structural power-dependence and social negotiation. Second, a study of the social desirability response bias underscored how the dual-process social psychological framework is important theoretically and the vignette experiment is important methodologically. Third, the study of the conditions under

 DOI:10.1163/9789004713918_008

which agency or communion have "primacy," buttressed the utility of both vignette experimentation and structural power-dependence theory. Fourth, the non-experimental exploratory study of female-male variation in implicit self-appraisal showed the continued explanatory value of the structural power-dependence framework as well as the strong potential of psycholinguistic analysis, using LIWC-22 as a valuable empirical research tool.

The research program traced in the present monograph might be effectively extended by following the basic strategy outlined in earlier chapters. While the original structural power-dependence formulation can serve as a fundamental point of departure, it can and should be flexibly extended by exploring and developing links to new and emerging lines of relevant research. Several promising lines of such research are briefly described below.

One important direction for future research is a deeper, more extensive exploration of potential links between structural power-dependence and the broad topic of *social negotiation.* How might the general process theory covered in the preceding chapters relate to studies undertaken by scholars pursuing more applied, concrete concerns such as politics, international affairs, diplomacy, and conflict resolution? Tracking answers to these questions might be useful.

For example, Zartman (2022) has reported an excellent in-depth analysis of historical cases concerned with the complex process through which power dynamics and a conflict over justice might or might not be resolved through negotiation. Potentially fruitful links might be drawn between his analysis and issues discussed in Chapter 2 above on justice norm formation in the context of structural power-dependence. Flexible, interdisciplinary work, joining insights from both structural power-dependence as a general process and particular historical analysis of cases such as that undertaken by Zartman should be encouraged and pursued. New sociological, political, and even diplomatic insights and applied policy interventions might well result.

Also, Richly, Hornung, and Bandelow (2021) have reported interesting research linking social identity theory (Tajfel, 2010) and the social negotiation of shared "storylines" in the process of (political) coalition formation. Clearly this work parallels the discussion in Chapter 2 above of "dialogical" (Markova, 1982; 2016) symbolic interaction dynamics entailed in coalition formation mobilized to change a power-dependence exchange network from a state of structural inequality toward structural equality and balanced power-dependence. It might well be fruitful to explore possible interconnections between general process theory-building/refining, on the one hand, and a more observational study of everyday political dynamics, such as the work reported by Rychly, Hornung, and Bendelow (2021), on the other.

In a similar vein, links should be explored between the literature reviewed by Van Dyke and Amos (2017) and structural power-dependence. These authors thoroughly examine "social movement coalition formation, longevity, and success … (identifying) five factors critical to coalition formation (a) social ties; (b) conducive organizational structures; (c) ideology, culture, and identity; (d) the institutional environment; and (e) resources" (Van Dyke and Amos, 2017:1). These five processes might be related to the dynamics of coalition formation discussed in Chapter 2 as well as cultural facets of exchange discussed in Chapter 3 of the present monograph. The conceptual parallels are striking, despite deriving from very different origins.

Another important direction for future research is an explicit evidence-based consideration of potential structural inequalities and biases that might come to shape aspects of the rapidly developing technology of *generative artificial intelligence*. Kuhlman, Jackson, and Chanara (2020) use the term, "algorithmic fairness" to capture the goal which they believe AI ought to strive to achieve. As these authors note, two fundamental threats to such fairness are (a) the fact that "…structural inequalities in our society are reflected in the data used to train predictive models and in the design of objective functions," and (b) the academic and corporate fields underlying AI development are themselves "under-represented" by people from diverse (ethnic, racial, and socioeconomic) backgrounds. Such threats must be squarely faced, accurately understood, and systematically addressed. Recent AI advances, including various AI GAs (e.g., OpenAI's ChatGPT, Google's Gemini, Perplexity's AI tool, and a number of others) are likely to bring many benefits to many people doing many complex tasks. Such developments will no doubt expand soon at an accelerating rate. However, it will be important for interdisciplinary research efforts to seek and publish clear accurate knowledge about how these developments might entail built-in biases that disadvantage some members of the society, and how such biases can be avoided. Interdisciplinary work such as that reported by Kuhlman, Jackson, and Chunara (2020) shows how the study of high technology and an understanding of structural power-dependence can combine to raise valuable questions that must be answered, going forward. Grappling with such questions will be essential in the future.

A different approach to potential threats and problems posed by generative AI is expressed by Kim (2022), who represents an explicitly legal approach to issues of structural inequality. As this scholar notes, "predictive AI" tools may bias the assessment of risk leading to unfair sentencing outcomes for people processed within the criminal justice system, may bias the chances of being recruited and hired for many kinds of jobs, and/or may bias various aspects of corporate management. The result may be unequal and unfair outcomes for many workers. In addition, some people may be unfairly denied credit by financial organizations due to biases underlying "predictive AI" assessments. It seems likely that various aspects of position-based structural inequality in social exchange networks of all kinds might well be exacerbated and rendered less transparent through the dramatic rise and use of AI.

In sum, "AI tools can contribute to inequality – both by reproducing discriminatory patterns that disadvantage marginalized groups, and by further concentrating power in ways that increase economic inequality" (Kim, 2022:19). A potentially useful direction for future research would be to link this legal perspective on the biases inherent in "predictive AI" to the perspective on structural power-dependence and inequality discussed in the present monograph. The results of such work, if they lead to appropriate regulatory policy, might potentially yield fairer outcomes for more people in various contexts, going forward.

"Social exchange theory" has long been and continues to be a valuable, widely used perspective for studying various forms of social behavior in many settings at different levels of analysis. This perspective yields important insights across the social sciences, including sociology, anthropology, psychology, political science, economics, international relations and history. The present monograph limited its focus to a single research program focused on structural power-dependence and social negotiation within social exchange networks. However, by showing how this program widened, how it became more inclusive, as it evolved, we have attempted to underscore the value of following an open, interdisciplinary research pathway forward. "Social exchange theory," whatever shape it takes, can continue to illuminate fundamental questions and crucial issues faced by society now and into the future.

References

Emerson, R.M. (1962) Power-Dependence Relations. *American Sociological Review* 27:31–40.

Emerson, R.M. (1969) Operant psychology and exchange theory. In R.L. Burgess and D. Bushel (eds.) Behavioral Sociology, Columbia University Press.

Emerson, R.M. (1972) Exchange theory: Parts I and II. In J. Berger, M. Zelditch, and B. Anderson (eds.) Sociological Theories in Progress, vol. 2, Houghton Mifflin.

Kim, P.T. (2022) AI and Inequality. In K. Johnson and C. Reyes (eds.) The Cambridge Handbook on Artificial Intelligence and The Law, Cambridge University Press.

Kuhlman, C., Jackson, L., and Chunara, R. (2020) No computation without representation: Avoiding data and algorithm biases through diversity. *ArXiv* 26 Feb.

Markova, I. (1982) Paradigms, Thought, and Language. Wiley.

Markova, I. (2016) The Dialogical Mind. Cambridge University Press.

Rychly, J., Hornung, J., and Bandelow, N.C. (2021) Come together, right now: storylines and social identities in coalition building in a local policy subsystem. *Politics and Policy* 49:1216–1247.

Stolte, J.F. and Emerson, R.M. (1977) Structural Inequality: Position and Power in Network Structures. In R. Hamblin and J. Kunkel, Behavioral Theory in Sociology. New York: Transaction Books.

Tajfel, H. (2010) Social Identity and Intergroup Relations. Cambridge University Press.

Van Dyke, N. and Amos, B. (2017) Social movement coalitions: Formation, Longevity, and Success. *Sociology Compass* e12489. https://doi.org/10.1111/soc4.12489.

Zartman, I.W. (2022) Justice in negotiating: How and where to find it and use it. *International Negotiation*. Online Publication Brill Publishers.

Index

www.ingramcontent.com/pod-product-compliance
Lightning Source LLC
LaVergne TN
LVHW010612110826
845149LV00003B/880
* 9 7 8 9 0 0 4 7 5 9 1 3 8 *